SEXUALLY TRANSMITTED DISEASES

D1508490

Other Books in the At Issue Series:

Affirmative Action
Anti-Semitism
Business Ethics
Child Labor and Sweatshops
Child Sexual Abuse
Cloning
Date Rape
Does Capital Punishment Deter Crime?
Domestic Violence
Environmental Justice
The Ethics of Euthanasia
Ethnic Conflict
The Future of the Internet
Gay Marriage
Immigration Policy
The Jury System
Legalizing Drugs
Marijuana
The Media and Politics
The Militia Movement
Physician-Assisted Suicide
Policing the Police
Rainforests
Rape on Campus
Sex Education
Single-Parent Families
Smoking
The Spread of AIDS
The United Nations
U.S. Policy Toward China
Voting Behavior
Welfare Reform
What Is Sexual Harassment?

SEXUALLY TRANSMITTED DISEASES

William Dudley, *Book Editor*

David L. Bender, *Publisher*
Bruno Leone, *Executive Editor*

Bonnie Szumski, *Editorial Director*
Scott Barbour, *Managing Editor*
Brenda Stalcup, *Series Editor*

An Opposing Viewpoints® Series

Greenhaven Press, Inc.
San Diego, California

Library of Congress Cataloging-in-Publication Data

Sexually transmitted diseases / William Dudley, book editor.
    p.   cm. — (At issue)
    Includes bibliographical references and index.
    ISBN 0-7377-0010-6 (pbk. : alk. paper). — ISBN 0-7377-0011-4
(lib. : alk. paper).
    1. AIDS (Disease)—Social aspects—United States. I. Dudley,
William, 1964– . II. Series: At issue (San Diego, Calif.).
RA644.A25S399   1999
616.95'1—dc21   98-38040
                                                                          CIP

©1999 by Greenhaven Press, Inc., PO Box 289009,
San Diego, CA 92198-9009

Printed in the U.S.A.

Every effort has been made to trace owners of copyrighted material.

Table of Contents

Page

Introduction   6

1. The United States Must Confront Its Epidemic of   8
   Sexually Transmitted Diseases
   Kaiser Family Foundation

2. Safer Sex Practices Can Be Satisfying and Prevent   13
   Sexually Transmitted Infections
   Planned Parenthood Federation of America

3. "Safe" Alternatives to Intercourse May Spread Sexually   22
   Transmitted Diseases
   Medical Institute for Sexual Health

4. Abstinence Education Can Prevent Sexually Transmitted   30
   Diseases
   Kathleen M. Sullivan

5. Abstinence-Only Sex Education Is Not Effective in   32
   Preventing Sexually Transmitted Diseases
   Center for AIDS Prevention Studies

6. Teenagers Should Be Taught About and Provided with   37
   Condoms
   M. Joycelyn Elders

7. Condoms Do Not Protect Teenagers from Sexually   40
   Transmitted Diseases
   John D. Hartigan

8. Bias and Discrimination Against Women Impede Efforts   44
   to Prevent Sexually Transmitted Diseases
   Hilary Hinds Kitasei

9. Concerns About Civil Rights Have Hobbled Efforts to   49
   Control AIDS
   Chandler Burr

10. Civil Rights Must Be Protected in the Fight Against AIDS   57
    American Civil Liberties Union

11. Gay Sexual Promiscuity Contributed to the AIDS Epidemic   70
    Gabriel Rotello

12. Gay Men Can Have Safe Sex and Avoid AIDS   83
    Joseph Sonnabend and Richard Berkowitz

Organizations to Contact   86

Bibliography   90

Index   93

Introduction

Sexually transmitted diseases (STDs), also called venereal diseases, are caused by germs that travel from person to person through sexual contact. Common STDs include syphilis, chlamydia, genital herpes, gonorrhea, and AIDS. Because the germs that cause STDs die quickly outside the human body, these sicknesses are not spread through coughing, sneezing, or contact with infected objects such as toilet seats or eating utensils. Most STDs, however, can be transmitted from an infected pregnant woman to her baby, often causing serious and life-threatening complications for the infant. Some viral diseases, including AIDS and hepatitis B, are spread through direct exposure to infected blood and can be transmitted through sexual contact or through nonsexual means such as the sharing of needles for drug use.

Sexually transmitted diseases have become a serious health problem in the United States. The Institute of Medicine, an arm of the National Academy of Sciences, asserts that STDs are prevalent and constitute a "hidden epidemic" because of the reluctance of Americans to "address sexual health issues in an open way." With twelve million new cases a year, America has one of the highest rates of STD infection in the industrialized world. STDs (including AIDS) cost the United States an estimated $17 billion in health care costs each year.

Chlamydia, a bacterial infection, is the most common sexually transmitted disease in the United States, affecting at least four million Americans annually. It is one of several STDs that can cause pelvic inflammatory disease—the inflammation of a woman's reproductive tract, which if left untreated can lead to infertility and death. The effects of other STDs vary. Genital herpes can create blistering and discomfort. The human papillomavirus (HPV) may cause cervical cancer. AIDS can fatally impair the body's immune system.

Young people are especially at risk for many sexually transmitted diseases. Teenagers account for three million cases of STDs annually. One out of every four sexually active teenagers acquires a new STD each year. One quarter of new infections of HIV (the virus that causes AIDS) are found in people under 22. Young women are at greater risk than older women for reproductive and health complications caused by STDs.

The medical options for the treatment and prevention of sexually transmitted diseases are somewhat limited. Some bacterial STDs, including chlamydia, syphilis, and gonorrhea, can be treated with antibiotics if detected early enough (although the evolution of new germs resistant to antibiotics is a growing problem). Antibiotics are useless against viral STDs, however. Public health measures have therefore focused primarily on preventing the spread of STDs. Because vaccinations for STDs are still in the research stage, efforts to prevent STDs have centered on reducing risky sexual activities. Yet while most people agree that healthy and responsible sexual behaviors should be promoted in the media, in clinics, and in sex education classes, profound disagreements exist as to what constitutes responsible behaviors.

For some people, responsible and disease-preventing behavior is synonymous with sexual restraint. They believe that everyone should be taught that abstaining from sex altogether or confining sex within a mutually monogamous relationship are the only 100 percent effective methods of keeping oneself free of all sexually transmitted diseases. Engaging in sex with multiple partners and relying on condoms to prevent STDs, in this view, is risky because condoms sometimes break, are not used properly, or are simply ineffective. Many advocates of abstinence criticize sex education programs in schools for including information on condoms and "safe sex," arguing that such a curriculum gives teenagers a false sense of security about sex and fails to discourage sexual activity. "To present 'protected' sex as an alternative to abstinence is inadequate," argues Joe S. McIlhaney, a gynecologist and founder of the Medical Institute for Sexual Health. "The best that 'safer sex' approaches can offer is some risk reduction. Abstinence, on the other hand, offers risk elimination. When the risks of pregnancy and disease are so great, even with contraception, how can we advocate anything less?"

Most people agree that abstinence is the most effective way of preventing sexually transmitted diseases and that people should be made aware that certain activities—including sex at an early age and sex with multiple partners or prostitutes—greatly increase the risks of contracting STDs. But many sex education authorities, such as Debra W. Haffner of the Sexuality Information and Education Council of the U.S., contend that abstinence should not be the sole emphasis of STD prevention and sex education programs. Americans should acknowledge that many teenagers are engaging in sexual activity, Haffner and others maintain. Studies have found that the average age of first intercourse in the United States is sixteen and that two-thirds of America's high school seniors are sexually experienced prior to graduation. Haffner argues that, given the reality that many teenagers reject the option of abstinence, young people should be given comprehensive sexuality information "about their bodies, gender roles, sexual abuse, pregnancy, and STD prevention," including the proper use of condoms to prevent diseases. She asserts that "fear-based, abstinence-only programs" that "discuss contraception only in negative terms" threaten to reverse "the significant strides American youth have made during the last two decades to delay sexual activity or else protect themselves."

Many of the viewpoints in *At Issue: Sexually Transmitted Diseases* reflect the differences between those who highlight sexual restraint and traditional values as imperative to preventing STDs and those who emphasize condom use and other methods of risk reduction. The relative merits of abstinence and condoms are among the several controversial issues discussed by the educators, health activists and organizations, and other contributors to this volume, all of whom present differing views on how best to stem the ongoing "hidden" epidemic of sexually transmitted diseases.

1

The United States Must Confront Its Epidemic of Sexually Transmitted Diseases

Kaiser Family Foundation

The Kaiser Family Foundation is a private philanthropic organization that supports research and public education projects on health-related issues.

The problem of sexually transmitted diseases (STDs) in the United States is serious and is underestimated by many health care professionals. Such diseases can cause serious complications, including infertility and death. Young people are especially at risk. Not all STDs are curable, but all are preventable. The United States needs a coordinated national system of health services and education campaigns on safe sexual behaviors to prevent the further spread of STDs.

What Are Sexually Transmitted Diseases (STDs) and How Many Different Types Are There?
"Sexually transmitted diseases" or "STDs" represent a group of at least 25 infectious organisms that are transmitted through sexual contact, and a number of syndromes that these STDs cause. These include: bacterial vaginosis, chancroid, chlamydia, cytomegalovirus (CMV), gonorrhea, hepatitis-B virus (HBV), herpes simplex virus (HSV) or genital herpes, human papillomavirus (HPV) or genital warts, hepatitis B, human immunodeficiency virus (HIV), pelvic inflammatory disease (PID), pubic lice, scabies, syphilis, and trichomoniasis. And, the number of STDs is growing. Since 1980, eight new sexually transmitted pathogens have been recognized in the United States alone, in part because technological advances have enabled scientists to detect and identify new infectious organisms and their associated syndromes.

Reprinted from *Sexually Transmitted Diseases in the United States: Exposing the Epidemic*, no. 1207 in the Q&A series published by the Kaiser Family Foundation, November 20, 1996. Reprinted with permission of the Henry J. Kaiser Family Foundation of Menlo Park, California. The Kaiser Family Foundation is an independent health care philanthropy and is not associated with Kaiser Permanente or Kaiser Industries.

Bacterial STDs, such as chlamydia, gonorrhea and syphilis, can be easily diagnosed and treated and are curable. Viral STDs, such as herpes, HPV and HIV, are incurable, but can be treated. All STDs are preventable.

The size of the crisis

How Prevalent Are STDs in the United States and in the Rest of the World?

Sexually transmitted diseases are at epidemic proportions in the United States, however, the scope of the epidemic and its impact is underestimated by the public and unacknowledged by many health care professionals. More than 12 million new cases of STDs, three million among teenagers, occur every year. At current rates, at least one person in four will contract an STD at some point in his or her life. Furthermore, as many as 56 million individuals—more than one in five Americans—may be infected with an incurable viral STD other than HIV, which causes AIDS.

STDs (excluding HIV/AIDS) are the second leading cause of mortality among healthy women of reproductive age (15–44) in the developing world, according to the World Bank. The World Health Organization (WHO) recently estimated that there were 333 million new cases of gonorrhea, chlamydia, syphilis and trichomoniasis worldwide in 1995 among adults ages 15–49. STD rates in the United States are the highest in the industrialized world, and are higher than in some developing countries.

Why Are STDs So Prevalent?

There are biological factors that contribute to the high rates of STDs, such as the lack of symptoms from some diseases in people, the lag time between initial infection and signs of complications, and women's increased susceptibility to STDs as compared to men's. Social factors such as poverty, lack of education, inadequate access to health care, substance and sexual abuse, and social inequity greatly increase the risk and prevalence of STDs in certain populations. Further, the ambivalence and mixed messages surrounding sexuality create barriers to STD prevention and control.

How Do We Know if STD Levels Are Rising? Is There a National System for STD Prevention and Control?

Although national surveillance and local information systems for STDs are critical to monitoring and evaluating trends in STDs, as well as to prevention efforts, current surveillance systems do not give accurate estimates of the incidence and prevalence of STDs in this country. Not all people with STDs obtain medical care and many of the services provided by private physicians for STD diagnosis and treatment go unreported. Consequently, the incidence and prevalence of most STDs are estimated and it is difficult to assess trends. As awareness grows and more people seek STD care, and health professionals recognize the importance of reporting, numbers may appear to increase.

Trends in viral STD infections, for example, are unknown. However, initial visits to doctors for genital warts and herpes have increased steadily over the last 30 years, dropping off slightly in the last 5 years. Nonetheless, it is clear from the limited trend data available that STDs represent a growing threat to the nation's health and well-being.

Who Are Affected Most by STDs? Are Some Groups of People at Higher Risk than Others?

STDs affect people of all racial, ethnic, cultural, social, economic, religious and age groups. People in all states and communities and social strata are at potential risk for acquiring an STD. Women, teenagers and minorities, however, are disproportionately affected by STDs. Women are biologically more susceptible to becoming infected if exposed to an STD, and STDs are more likely to remain undetected in women, resulting in delayed diagnosis and treatment. As a result, women are also more likely to develop certain, and more severe, complications if infected with an STD.

Young people are hit hardest by STDs. Three million teenagers—about one in four sexually experienced teenagers—acquire an STD every year. Teenagers are at high risk for acquiring an STD because they are more likely to have multiple partners, unprotected sex, and exposure to infected partners.

In a single act of unprotected sex with an infected partner, a teenage woman has a 1% risk of acquiring HIV. She has a 30% risk of getting genital herpes, and a 50% chance of contracting gonorrhea. Chlamydia and gonorrhea are more common among teenagers than among older men and women. In some studies, up to 15% of sexually active teenage women have been found to be infected with HPV, many with a strain of this virus that is linked to cervical cancer. Teenage women have the highest rate of hospitalization for acute pelvic inflammatory disease, most often caused by untreated gonorrhea or chlamydia, which can lead to infertility and ectopic pregnancy. Through 1995, over two thousand teenagers and 93,000 men and women in their twenties (who most likely contracted HIV as a teenager) were known to have AIDS.

STD rates vary among ethnic and racial groups, with a higher prevalence of some STDs (such as chlamydia, gonorrhea and syphilis) among African-Americans and Latinos as compared to whites. The reasons for these higher rates are not clear, however, some explanations cite factors such as socioeconomic status and problems accessing health care.

Sexually transmitted diseases are at epidemic proportions in the United States.

What Are the Health and Economic Consequences of STDs?

STDs place an enormous health burden on Americans. The health consequences of STDs affecting millions of women, infants and men range from mild illnesses to serious long-term consequences including: various cancers, reproductive health problems such as infertility, ectopic pregnancy and spontaneous abortion, other chronic illnesses, and even death. Incurable viral STDs, such as HPV and herpes, result in lifelong infection and complications. STD infections increase susceptibility to HIV, and also increase HIV infectiousness. People who have an active syphilis, genital herpes, or chancroid infection, or who have chlamydia, gonorrhea, or trichomoniasis are 3 to 5 times more likely to contract HIV than other people.

The public and private costs of STDs are substantial, as well. The Institute of Medicine (IOM) convened a 15-member expert Committee on Prevention and Control of Sexually Transmitted Diseases which examined the scope of STDs in this country and the factors contributing to their epidemic proportions; assessed the effectiveness of current public health campaigns and programs to prevent and control STDs; and provided recommendations for public health program planning, policymaking and research addressing STD prevention and control. In their report, *The Hidden Epidemic: Confronting Sexually Transmitted Diseases* (released November 19, 1996), the Committee conservatively estimates that in 1994 the total annual costs associated with major STDs and their related syndromes—chlamydia, gonorrhea, PID, syphilis, chancroid, herpes, HPV, hepatitis B and cervical cancer—are about $10 billion, and $17 billion when sexually transmitted HIV/AIDS infections are included.

An effective national system for STD protection and control does not currently exist in this country.

Do Health Insurance Plans Address Concerns About Confidentiality in STD Testing and Treatment?

Practices to protect patient confidentiality vary among health plans.

• Seventy-one percent of HMOs [health maintenance organizations] allow a spouse or other dependent (who is at least age 18) to receive confidential services without having to obtain the employee's signature on the claim form; 64% accord confidentiality to dependents younger than 18.

• Only 10% of point-of-service networks and 12% of preferred provider organizations provide a routine explanation-of-benefits form, which identifies both patient and provider, directly to the dependent; the remainder require the involvement of the employee.

• One out of eight managed care plans (13%) provide special protection, above and beyond normal confidentiality measures, for the confidentiality of their patients' records if they have sought diagnosis and treatment for sexually transmitted diseases.

• Only 2% of plans have separate billing procedures for STD services in order to protect patient confidentiality.

• Most managed care plans do not require parental consent or notification for providing STD testing and treatment to teens (under 18 years old): 3% of plans say they require parental consent and 2% say they require parental notification to offer teens these services.

Recommendations for reform

How Can the United States Better Fight the STD Epidemic?

The Institute of Medicine Committee also concluded that an effective national system for STD protection and control does not currently exist in this country, resulting in an STD prevalence that is the highest in the industrialized world. Their overarching recommendation was for the nation to develop "an effective system of services and information that supports individuals, families, and communities, in preventing STDs including HIV, and ensures comprehensive, high-quality STD-related health services for all persons." The committee set forth a number of strategic goals to:

• Develop strong leadership, strengthen investment, and improve information systems for STD prevention and control;

• Overcome barriers to adoption of healthy sexual behaviors by promoting knowledge and awareness, minimizing conflicting mass media messages, improving professionals' skills in sexual health issues, and supporting health behavior research;

• Design and implement essential STD-related services in innovative ways for adolescents and underserved populations by focusing on prevention, focusing on adolescents and establishing new venues for interventions; and,

• Ensure access to essential clinical services for STDs, by ensuring access to services in the community, improving the quality of dedicated public STD clinics, involving health plans and purchasers of health care, improving training and education of health care professionals, and improving clinical management of STDs.

Changing the sexual behaviors that spread STDs is essential for prevention. Open communication and sexuality education play important roles in changing attitudes toward establishing healthier, less risky sexual behavior. Other important steps toward preventing STDs are making informed decisions about sex, such as avoiding sex with an infected person and using condoms consistently and correctly.

Sources of Information:

GHAA/Kaiser Family Foundation Survey of Reproductive Health Benefits, 1994.

The Hidden Epidemic: Confronting Sexually Transmitted Diseases, Institute of Medicine, National Academy Press, 1996.

Improving the Fit: Reproductive Health Services in Managed Care Settings, The Alan Guttmacher Institute, 1996.

Testing Positive: Sexually Transmitted Disease and the Public Health Response, The Alan Guttmacher Institute, 1993.

2

Safer Sex Practices Can Be Satisfying and Prevent Sexually Transmitted Infections

Planned Parenthood Federation of America

Planned Parenthood Federation of America is a national organization of medical clinics that provide medical, counseling, and educational services relating to sexual and reproductive health, including screening and treatment for sexually transmitted diseases.

Sex is a normal and enjoyable part of life, but it carries with it the risk of contracting sexually transmitted infections (STIs). "Safer sex" refers to various techniques that sexually active people can utilize in order to lower their risks of contracting such diseases. By using condoms and practicing alternatives to intercourse, such as mutual masturbation, people can avoid contact with their sexual partner's body fluids. Practicing safer sex can actually broaden and enhance a person's sex life in addition to preventing disease.

> *"My love life actually improved when I started having safer sex."*
> *—a 41-year-old Hispanic man.*

E njoying Sex Is a Normal, Natural Part of Life.
We are all sexual—from birth to death. When we decide to have sex, we want it to be satisfying—whether we're women or men, married or single, young or old, straight, lesbian, gay, or bisexual.

Most of us have taken risks to have sex—risks that include sexually transmitted infections (STIs). We take so many risks that at least one out of four of us becomes infected some time in our lives.

The risks we take can be dangerous. Many sexually transmitted infections:

- last a lifetime
- put stress on relationships
- cause sterility
- cause birth defects
- lead to major illness and death.

Adapted with permission from *Sex—Safer and Satisfying*, by Planned Parenthood® Federation of America, Inc. © Revised version 1997 PPFA. All rights reserved.

We know that safer sex reduces our risks. But many of us don't make the effort, because we think safer sex will be less satisfying. It does not have to be. Some of us think safer sex is only about condoms. It's not. We may think it's only about AIDS. It's not. Safer sex is about a lot more. It's also about sexual pleasure.

Exploring safer sex can make sex more satisfying. It can:

- improve partner communication
- increase intimacy and trust
- prolong sex play
- enhance orgasm
- add variety to sexual pleasure
- relieve anxiety
- strengthen relationships.

> *"I like sex a lot—some people would call me promiscuous. But I know how to handle myself. I don't do anything to let anyone's body fluids inside my body. And I get tested every year to be sure I don't pass anything along to someone else. Except for a case of crabs two years ago, I haven't had an STI in 10 years. I can tell you from experience—safer sex works."*
>
> —*a 35-year-old white woman.*

What is safer sex?

Safer sex is anything we do to lower our risks of getting an STI.

It's about getting more pleasure with less risk.

Three Steps to Safer Sex

- Become honest with ourselves about the risks we take.
- Decide which risks we are willing to take—and which ones we aren't willing to take.
- Find ways to make our safer sex play as satisfying as possible.

The most important way to reduce your risk is to keep your partner's body fluids out of your body.

The body fluids to be most careful about are blood, cum, pre-cum, vaginal fluids, and the discharges from sores caused by STIs.

There Are Only Two Basic Rules

- Keep your partner's body fluids out of your vagina, anus, and mouth.
- Don't touch sores that are caused by STIs.

Safer sex also means protecting your partner, so return the favor.

- Don't allow your body fluids to get into your partner's body.
- Don't have sex if you have sores or other STI symptoms.
- Get checked for STIs every year, and get the correct treatment if you become infected.

Unprotected vaginal and anal intercourse have the highest risks for the most dangerous STIs. Lower-risk sex play includes:

- Masturbation
- Mutual Masturbation
- Outercourse
- Erotic Massage
- Body Rubbing

- Kissing
- Deep Kissing
- Oral Sex
- Vaginal Intercourse with a Male or Female Condom
- Anal Intercourse with a Male or Female Condom.

> *"I always hoped that someday I'd be able to share my life and enjoy sex with only one special partner. In the meantime, I insisted on safer sex with the partners I had. Now that I've found my partner for life, I'm really glad I played it safe."*
> —*27-year-old African-American man.*

Is It Safe to Have Sex With Only One Partner?

Maybe. The ideal for many people is to have sex with only one partner. Women and men don't need to worry about getting STIs:

- if neither partner ever had sex with anyone else
- if neither partner ever shared needles
- if neither partner was ever infected.

Safer sex reduces our risks.

Most of us have more than one sex partner during our lives. We may not plan it that way, but it happens. We may also get an infection from one partner and carry it to another. The partners who gave it to us:

- may not have known they were infected
- may have *hoped* they wouldn't infect us
- may not have been totally honest about their sexual history.

Some of us have only one partner, but our partner may "cheat." Most women who got HIV from having sex thought they were their sex partners' only sex partners.

You and your sex partner may want to give up safer sex because you've decided to have sex with no one else. Before you do, be sure that neither of you is infected. Some infections, like HIV, may take years to develop symptoms. You may not even know they are there. See your local Planned Parenthood or health care provider and get yourself checked out for STIs.

> *"Whether or not my partners have HIV isn't important. I know it's up to me to protect myself. I don't take anyone's word for it until we've been through an awful lot together, and even then, I'm careful. They have to be careful, too, or they get no loving from me."*
> —*a 25-year-old white woman.*

Whom Can We Trust?

Many of us know how it feels to discover that a sex partner has been dishonest with us. More than one out of three people will lie about their feelings to have sex with someone else. A similar number will lie about their sexual history. The same number will lie about whether or not they have HIV!

When it comes to safer sex, rely on yourself. Believing you are your sex partner's only sex partner will not make it true. Here are some questions to think over:

- Do I know how my partner spends time away from me?
- Is my partner always open about everything with me?
- Does my partner get upset if I want to have a "serious" talk about our relationship?
- Does my partner keep secrets from me?
- Does my partner ever say, "I'm just going out" or "It's none of your business"?
- Is my partner always respectful to me?

We all want partners we can trust. The key is to make sure that our partners earn our trust. We should never just give it away.

> *"I got hepatitis B years ago. I'm still a carrier and can't drink wine anymore. These days there's a vaccine so no one has to get this disease."*
>
> —*a 52-year-old white man.*

Not All STIs Are Transmitted the Same Way.

You need to know a little bit about how you might get an STI. Here are the basics about your risks:

IF YOU HAVE UNPROTECTED VAGINAL OR ANAL INTERCOURSE YOU ARE AT HIGH RISK FOR

- trichomoniasis
- gonorrhea
- chlamydia
- syphilis
- chancroid
- human papilloma viruses (HPVs) that can cause genital warts
- herpes simplex virus (HSV) that can cause genital herpes
- pelvic inflammatory disease (PID) that can cause sterility
- hepatitis B virus (HBV)
- cytomegalovirus (CMV)
- pubic lice
- scabies
- human immunodeficiency virus (HIV) that can cause AIDS.

IF YOU HAVE UNPROTECTED ORAL SEX YOU ARE AT HIGH RISK FOR

- gonorrhea
- syphilis
- chancroid
- HSV
- HBV
- CMV.

IF YOU HAVE SEX PLAY WITHOUT SEXUAL INTERCOURSE YOU ARE AT RISK FOR

- HSV
- CMV
- HPV
- pubic lice
- scabies.

Lots of other diseases, from the flu to mononucleosis, can also be transmitted sexually.

"Everybody is different. Everyone has to decide what risks they are prepared to take—then decide what to do."
—*a 26-year-old African-America woman.*

If You Are A Woman . . .
Your risk of getting an STI is greater than a man's. Your vagina and rectum are more easily infected than his penis. A woman's chance of being infected by a man with HIV is twice as great as a man's chance of being infected by a woman with HIV.

Women generally have fewer symptoms than men. You are less likely to know if you are infected. Lots of damage can be done, even if you have no symptoms. Many women develop PID because they don't know they have an STI. PID increases the risk of sterility and ectopic pregnancy.

"At first, I put off intercourse with new partners by having sex without penetration. I wouldn't have intercourse until I knew them better and could be sure they would use a condom right. Now, I'm really into sex without intercourse. It's hot."
—*a 35-year-old African-American woman.*

Sex can be very satisfying without intercourse

Great sex is about a lot more than penetration with a penis. It's about exploring the many ways you can turn your partner on. It's exploring the many ways that you can be turned on. It's about finding new turnons and rediscovering old ones.

You don't have to be shy about your sexual pleasure. Partners who explore safer sex with one another may discover new sexual excitements. They can be clear about how and where they like to be caressed. They help one another enjoy sex even more.

Sex Play Without Penetration Is Called Outercourse

A lot of people have vaginal intercourse because they think they're *supposed* to. For a long time, women and men were taught that "good sex" only meant having an orgasm during vaginal intercourse. Nothing could be less true.

Most women don't have orgasms from vaginal stimulation. Most of them get orgasms when the clitoris is stimulated—whether or not they are being penetrated by a penis. Men also enjoy outercourse—even if they're shy about letting their partners know.

Outercourse with many partners can be safer than intercourse with only one.

"Safer sex taught me how to be more erotic—how to enjoy my body and my partner's body without worry or embarrassment."
—*a 21-year-old Asian man.*

Outercourse—Alternatives to Intercourse
Masturbation
Masturbation is the most common way we enjoy sex. Partners can enjoy it together while hugging and kissing or watching one another. Mas-

turbating together can deepen a couple's intimacy.

Erotic Massage

Many couples enjoy arousing one another with body massage. They stimulate each other's sex organs with their hands, bodies, or mouths. They take turns bringing each other to orgasm.

Body Rubbing

Many couples rub their bodies together, especially their sex organs, for intense sexual pleasure.

Erotica, Fantasy, Role Play, Masks

Reading, watching, or telling erotic fantasies with a sex partner can be very exciting. Acting out fantasies can be exciting, too. Masks and costumes may intensify this kind of sex play.

Sex Toys

Sex toys, including vibrators and dildos, can also heighten sexual pleasure. They are used to stroke, stimulate, probe, and caress the body.

It's very important to keep sex toys clean—especially if they are shared during sex play. Condoms can be used to cover toys that are inserted into the body. Use a fresh condom for each partner and each part of the body.

> *"The woman I love has herpes—she told me on our first date— so we deal with it. I always wear a condom, and when she has an outbreak, we catch up on the latest movies."*
>   —*a 37-year-old Hispanic man.*

Condoms Are the Best Protection for Enjoying Sexual Intercourse.
Condoms help make sex last longer.
Condoms help prevent premature ejaculation.
Latex and female condoms offer good protection against:
- vaginitis caused by trichomoniasis
- honeymoon cystitis
- PID
- gonorrhea
- chlamydia
- syphilis
- chancroid
- HIV/AIDS.

Latex and female condoms offer some protection against:

Safer Sex and Birth Control

Remember: Most forms of birth control do not protect against STIs.

Use a male or female condom every time you have vaginal intercourse—even if you use:

• the Pill • Norplant® • Depo-Provera® • IUD • diaphragm
• cervical cap • predicting fertility methods • withdrawal
• foam • cream • jelly • film • suppository

. . . even if you are sterilized.

Spermicide offers some protection against chlamydia, gonorrhea, and trichomoniasis. Do not rely on it to protect against viruses like HIV, HSV, and HPV.

- genital warts
- herpes
- hepatitis-B virus.

How to use condoms

Don't tear the condom while unwrapping it.

Don't use one that's brittle, stiff, or sticky.

Use plenty of water-based lubricant. It helps prevent rips and tears, and it increases sensitivity. Oil-based lubricants destroy latex condoms.

Use a condom only once.

Have a good supply on hand.

Practice makes perfect!

- Put a drop or two of lubricant inside the condom.
- Place the rolled condom over the tip of the hard penis.
- Leave a half-inch space at the tip to collect semen.
- If not circumcised, pull back the foreskin before rolling on the condom.
- Pinch the air out of the tip with one hand. (Friction against air bubbles causes most condom breaks.)
- Unroll the condom over the penis with the other hand.
- Roll it all the way down to the base of the penis.
- Smooth out any air bubbles.
- Lubricate the outside of the condom.

ENJOY!

- Pull out before the penis softens.
- Don't spill the semen—hold the condom against the base of the penis while you pull out.

The Female Condom Also Protects Against STIs.

The female condom is a polyurethane sheath with a flexible ring at each end. It is inserted deep into the vagina like a diaphragm. It stays in place even if a guy loses his erection.

Condoms can be used for protection during oral sex on men. Cut-open condoms, dental dams, and plastic wrap provide protection during oral sex on women. Do not use male and female condoms together.

> *"It was when I realized that I didn't have to get high to have sex that I really began to enjoy myself. I realized I didn't need to take the risks I was taking to have a good time. Feeling better about sex makes me feel better about myself."*
> —*a 65-year-old white woman.*

Many People Have Mixed Feelings About Sex.

As much as we like sex, it embarrasses a lot of us. Sometimes we can't admit we enjoy it. Some of us use alcohol or other drugs to feel less self-conscious about enjoying ourselves. But drugs also encourage us to take risks we wouldn't take if we weren't high.

- alcohol

- speed
- acid
- marijuana
- cocaine
- poppers
- crack
- ecstasy
- downers
- heroin

The more we use drugs when we have sex, the more we are likely to take risks.

We also have a lot of feelings that encourage taking risks with sex. They include:

- Passion
- Desire to Be Swept Away
- Fear of Losing a Partner
- Desire to Be Attractive
- Low Self-Esteem
- Need to Be Wanted
- Shame
- Embarrassment
- Insecurity
- Anger
- Shyness
- Grief

Women and men who are comfortable with their sexuality are more likely to enjoy safer sex.

Exploring safer sex can make sex more satisfying.

If drug use, shame, or other feelings block your safer sex plans, make an appointment to talk with a sexual health counselor. A counselor can help you work through the feelings that keep you from having safer sex—for confidential counseling or referral, call your nearest Planned Parenthood at 1-800-230-PLAN.

> *"For me, the scariest STI is HIV. I volunteered for my local AIDS service organization to get over my fear. Being a buddy for someone with AIDS taught me a lot. One of the things it taught me was how important safer sex is. I started being very careful after my first client died. I hope other people don't wait as long as I did."*
> *—a 24-year-old Hispanic woman.*

Am I Ready for Safer Sex?

A Self-Assessment Quiz

T   F   I want to be able to let my partner know where and how I like to be touched.

T   F   I want to be able to buy condoms, whether I'm embarrassed or not.

T   F   If I decide I want to use erotic materials, I want to be able to buy them myself—whether I'm embarrassed or not.

T   F   I want to be able to let my partner know my limits when it comes to taking risks.

T   F   I want to be able to say no to sex when I don't want to have it.

T   F   I want to have regular physical exams and checkups for STIs.

T   F   I want to be able to talk with my clinician about my sex life.

T   F   I want to be able to enjoy sex without having to get high.

If you answered "True" to more than half of these questions, you are well on your way to becoming assertive enough for safer sex. Congratulations!

3

"Safe" Alternatives to Intercourse May Spread Sexually Transmitted Diseases

Medical Institute for Sexual Health

The Medical Institute for Sexual Health is a medical education organization that provides health information to parents, students, and educators that emphasizes the consequences of irresponsible sexual involvement.

Some public health leaders and organizations maintain that mutual masturbation and other forms of "outercourse" are safe alternatives to penetrative sex and that young people should be taught about these options as a means of reducing the incidence of sexually transmitted diseases (STDs). However, medical researchers have found that the organisms that cause STDs are present in the sexual secretions of men and women and can be transmitted from one person to another by sexual activity that does not include vaginal or anal intercourse. Educators should not teach adolescents that mutual masturbation and similar activities can protect them from STDs. Instead, they should challenge young people to limit sex to lifelong monogamous relationships.

Former Surgeon General Joycelyn Elders lost her job when she recommended that sexuality education include teaching students about masturbation. On World AIDS Day, December 1, 1994, at a meeting of the Society for the Psychological Study of Social Issues in New York City, Dr. Elders answered a question from Dr. Rob Clark about masturbation education by replying, "As for your specific question about masturbation, I think it is something that is part of human sexuality and is part of something that perhaps should be taught."[1]

When the Surgeon General and several nationally recognized sex edu-

Reprinted from "Masturbation, Mutual Masturbation, Outercourse, and Dry Sex," *Sexual Health Update*, vol. 3, no. 1 (March 1995), a publication of the Medical Institute for Sexual Health, by permission of the publisher.

cation organizations refer to "masturbation," to what activity are they referring? The definition in *Dorland's Medical Dictionary*, 28th Edition, 1994, says that masturbation is "self-stimulation of the genitals for sexual pleasure." "Mutual masturbation" is a term used by sex educators and others to refer to stimulation of another person's genital organs for sexual pleasure. "Outercourse" is defined as genital contact without penetrative sex, either oral, anal, or vaginal. This is the same sexual activity that is commonly referred to with the slang term, "dry sex." Whether Dr. Elders was referring to all of these forms of masturbation or not, we do not know. We do know that several national organizations which are being taken quite seriously by educators are advocating that children be taught about the full range of masturbatory activity. The subject of this article is mutual masturbation and outercourse. Therefore, we will not discuss self masturbation.

The primary question about mutual masturbation and outercourse is, "Are they medically acceptable, safe alternatives to penetrative sex for individuals in our society who might otherwise be at risk of becoming pregnant or of becoming infected with a sexually transmitted disease if they participated in penetrative sex?" Before we answer that, it is important that we consider the act itself. Many people who are involved in sexual activity for the first time are surprised that it is such a "messy" activity. The culmination of sexual activity for a man is ejaculation of semen, a wet sticky fluid. For a woman, "The first sign of sexual excitation in the female is the appearance of vaginal lubrication which starts ten to thirty seconds after the onset of sexual stimulation—which may be physical, psychological, or a combination of the two."[2] If a woman is masturbating a man, her hands will be covered with his semen when he ejaculates. When a man masturbates a woman, his hands will become quite moist with her vaginal secretions. It is quite likely that at some time during this sexual activity the people involved will touch their own genitals with their moist hands.

Transmission of sexually transmitted disease from one person to another may occur when contaminated sexual secretions are transmitted from one person to another, whether or not penetrative sex has occurred. The medical issue which concerns us in regard to mutual masturbation is whether sexual secretions contain sexually transmitted disease organisms. If the sexual secretions of the man or of the woman contain sexually transmitted disease organisms, they can be transmitted to a sexual partner even without penetrative sex because no area of the body is totally protected from such infection. (For example, a dentist can get herpes of his/her finger from exposure to oral secretions from a patient with herpes of the lip.)

STD organisms in semen

We will review some research which supports the presence of sexually transmitted disease organisms in semen.

1. Human papillomavirus (HPV) J. Green and co-workers found, in a study reported in *Genitourinary Medicine* in 1991, that they could detect HPV DNA in 85% of semen specimens from men attending a clinic for treatment of genital warts.[3] A subgroup of men studied had warts just inside the urethra. In this location the man would not know he had warts, and the woman would have no way of knowing he was infected with warts. All the semen collected from these men with warts just inside the urethral opening contained HPV organisms. Ninety-five percent of these men also had a second HPV organism present. Therefore, most men who have genital warts will have the wart virus present in their semen. A woman can become infected in those areas of her body which come in contact with his semen. It is important to note that HPV is the most common sexually transmitted virus in the U.S. today.

Many people who are involved in sexual activity for the first time are surprised that it is such a "messy" activity.

---

2. HIV (the AIDS virus) Ilaria and co-workers reported, in an article in *The Lancet*, a British medical journal, in December 1992, that many men who are HIV positive have the virus in their pre-ejaculatory fluid.[4] They said, "Specimens from six of the fourteen men, 43 percent, tested repeatedly positive for HIV-1 DNA." They then said, "Since exposure to pre-ejaculatory fluid may occur during sexual intercourse or genital contact, this fluid may be a vector for transmission of HIV-1 infections if the virus is present." It might be helpful to explain that when men are sexually excited, they will often have a small amount of secretions from the penis. This occurs before actual ejaculation. These secretions are called pre-ejaculatory fluid, and, as mentioned in this article, can be infected with HIV. Other studies have shown that semen of men who are HIV-positive does carry a great deal of the virus.

This issue was chillingly demonstrated by Knobel, in an article he wrote in the *South African Medical Journal* in 1988.[5] He entitled the article "Urgent Warning of Contraction of HIV Infection During Mutual Masturbation." In this article he discussed two men who mutually masturbated. One of the men would rub his partner's semen over his own penis which had skin breakdown because of "penile pressure." The man who did this contracted HIV infection from his partner.

3. Hepatitis C Kotwal studied men who were infected with hepatitis C.[6] All nine of the patients he studied who were infected with hepatitis C showed signs of that virus in their semen. To be complete, he studied five healthy semen donors, none of whom had hepatitis C present in their semen. He concluded, "This more direct evidence for viral presence supports the earlier epidemiological data suggesting that HCV (hepatitis C) could be transmitted sexually."

4. Chlamydia Chlamydia is present in semen. Chlamydia, as a matter of fact, can be difficult to detect in men. A.J.C. van den Brule and co-workers, in *Fertility and Sterility* in 1993, reported startling findings when they studied semen donors.[7] The semen donors had already been cultured for chlamydia and found to be negative. It was assumed that they were acceptable for semen donation for fertility clinics. When DNA testing for chlamydia was done on the semen of thirty of the donors, it was found that three out of the thirty donors (10%) did have chlamydia in their semen and therefore could infect women who were inseminated with their sperm.

Women's secretions and STDs

Do women's secretions carry the organisms that cause sexually transmitted disease? We will review some data concerning women.

   1. *HPV* A study of sexually active coeds at the University of California at Berkeley showed that 46 percent were infected with HPV.[8] The tests were taken by swabbing the vagina of each woman who was part of the study.

   2. *Herpes* R.W. Cone and co-workers reported in the *Journal of the American Medical Association* in 1994.[9] These researchers studied women in labor who did not have visible herpes. They took secretions from the vaginas and cervices of these women with swabs. They found that of 100 women in labor who did not have any history of herpes outbreaks at all, nine had actual herpes virus present.

   STD testing for women is typically done by swabbing the vulvar, vaginal, and cervical tissues, just as Cone and his co-workers did with their herpes study. If a woman has a sexually transmitted disease, therefore, she will usually have the organisms which cause that disease present in her secretions. Because of this, these diseases can be transmitted to a man if he comes in contact with those secretions, even if he does not have penetrative intercourse with her.

   Can pregnancy occur without vaginal sex? Clearly this can happen. Sperm have the capacity to swim up the vaginal canal, through the cervix, and into the uterus to produce a pregnancy. Sperm can do this whether they are deposited high in the vagina or at the vaginal entrance. If mutual masturbation occurs in such a way that semen is deposited at the woman's vaginal entrance, she does run the risk of becoming pregnant. Outercourse ("dry sex"), which does involve close genital contact, obviously can result in a man's ejaculation at a woman's vaginal entrance and, therefore, be the cause of pregnancy, even though the woman may still be a virgin.

   The medical literature has many articles such as the ones we have quoted. If a person has a sexually transmitted disease, the organisms will usually be present in that person's sexual secretions. These secretions can be passed to a partner during the act of mutual masturbation or during the act of outercourse.

Teaching young people about safe sex

In spite of this very clear medical data, organizations such as SIECUS (Sexuality Information and Education Council of the U.S.) and Planned Parenthood recommend that young people be taught that mutual masturbation and outercourse are acceptable and safe sexual practices. In their *Guidelines for Comprehensive Sexuality Education*, SIECUS recommends that Level Three students, whom they define as early adolescents, ages 12–15, middle school/high school, be taught about masturbation. They say, "Masturbation, either alone or with a partner, is one way a person can enjoy and express their sexuality without risking pregnancy or an STD/HIV."[10] For Level Four students, whom they define as adolescents, ages 15–19, high school, they recommend education that includes, "Some common sexual behaviors shared by partners include kissing, touching, caressing, massaging, sharing erotic literature or art, bathing/showering together, and/or oral, vaginal, or anal intercourse."[11]

Most parents and teachers would probably assume that a national organization which advocates this type of education would be merely a fringe group in the spectrum of organizations which are involved in sex education. This is not the case. SIECUS recommends these sex education guidelines for all schools in the U.S. and is actually being taken seriously by some adults in policy making positions. "In March 1994 SIECUS was awarded a cooperative agreement with the Centers for Disease Control, Prevention Division of Adolescent School of Health, under the National Program to Strengthen Comprehensive School Health Programs. SIECUS will be developing several projects designed to promote comprehensive sexuality and HIV/AIDS education as a priority in the nation's schools. The following projects are included in this program—regional conferences, state curricula and guidelines for HIV/AIDS education, and recognition of model programs."[12]

Disease organisms . . . can be transmitted to a sexual partner even without penetrative sex.

Planned Parenthood advocates the same education. In a booklet written by Planned Parenthood for parents entitled *How To Talk With Your Teen About The Facts Of Life* they state, "Safest sex (no sexual intercourse)—masturbation, mutual masturbation, touching, massaging, body rubbing, kissing, deep kissing or biting without bruising, oral sex on a man with a condom, oral sex on a woman with a dental dam or plastic wrap. (Don't worry about: cum on unbroken skin away from the vulva; vaginal secretions or menstrual flow on unbroken skin; urine on unbroken skin.)"[13]

It is of concern that a nationally recognized organization would encourage parents to teach their children about this activity and ignore the very significant risks of both pregnancy and sexually transmitted disease.

There are a number of problems with educating young people to participate in mutual masturbation or outercourse:

1. It is dangerous and dishonest sex education if the implication is that STD and pregnancy can be avoided with this activity. Disease organisms can survive in moist conditions outside the body long enough for infection to occur. Although not highly likely, pregnancy is also possible.
2. Adults and youth alike misunderstand mutual masturbation. Many young people, for example, would not realize that mutual masturbation does not include oral/genital sexual activity. They do not understand that oral/genital sexual activity is sex which includes a great risk for the spread of sexually transmitted disease.
3. Many people do not understand the significance of broken skin. They do not realize that a small crack or cut in the skin can be an entry way for sexually transmitted disease into the body, even if it is on the hands or the inner part of the thighs and even if it is not noticeable.

4. It is naive to assume that anyone participating in mutual masturbation will not progress very rapidly to penetrative sex. This type of sexual activity is for the preparation of one's partner for penetrative sex. This is the reason it has been, in the past, called "foreplay." Foreplay is for the purpose of increasing the sexual tension between two people so they will then progress into penetrative sexual intercourse.

5. A broader issue is that studies clearly show that the teaching of medical facts does not decrease the incidence of pregnancy or sexually transmitted disease for teenagers. Many medical articles have been written about this subject. The latest was in the February 1995 issue of *Obstetrics and Gynecology*, which states there is "no link, either positive or negative, between knowledge of reproductive biology and age of first intercourse."[14] Studies are showing very clearly that young people must be taught to avoid sexual activity and must be taught good character traits in order to develop the personal strength of character necessary to delay sexual activity until later, the best choice they have for staying sexually and physically healthy.

Teaching about sexual activity of this type in classrooms of junior high and high school students sends a very loud message to them that their teachers, who are teaching this material, and their parents, who are allowing this material to be taught in the schools, think that they can have this type of sexual activity safely and appropriately.

Two stories

In conclusion, consider the sad stories of two young women. Two physician friends sent these reports to the Medical Institute for Sexual Health.

The first is the case of "a 13-year-old girl, who adamantly reported that she had never had sex, who was evaluated for vulvar skin changes. On exam, she appeared to be virginal, as reported, but her vulvar skin biopsy showed VIN III (precancer that has almost advanced to invasive cancer). She reported that she had participated in what is called 'outercourse' with her boy friend. We performed laser surgery on her vulva for treatment. On follow up about eight to nine months later, she had carcinoma in situ of the vulva (which is a step even closer to cancer of the vulva), at which time she underwent removal of her vulvar skin with grafting of skin from her buttocks. Aesthetically, her vulva is changed forever and will never appear normal."

Adults and youth alike misunderstand mutual masturbation.

A second case is the following: "Here are the details on that case I told you about with gonococcal arthritis. This is a 15-year-old female who was admitted to the emergency room with a two day history of increasing pain in her right knee, right foot, and ankle. She was examined in the ER by a female emergency room physician who felt that she had a virginal introitus (that she had never had penetrative sexual intercourse). There was a high suspicion of gonococcal infection, and therefore, cultures were taken including aspiration of her knee. Ultimately, Neisseria gonorrhoeae (the germ that causes gonorrhea) was, in fact, grown from the knee aspirate. She was treated with IV antibiotics."

These and other studies clearly show that sexual secretions contain the sexually transmitted organisms which infect people with sexually transmitted disease. These infections can occur whether or not penetrative sex has occurred. It is very poor scholarship for nationally recognized sex education organizations such as SIECUS, Planned Parenthood, and others, to advocate mutual masturbation and outercourse as safe sexual activity. Our young people deserve better than to have subjects such as this taught in their classrooms. They should be protected from this kind of education, because it is erroneous, and, therefore, dangerous. It is also inappropriate. It leads them to the brink of penetrative sexual intercourse, which carries with it even greater risk of disease. They deserve more. We can and should challenge our young people to learn how to say no to sex until they enter into a lifelong, mutually monogamous, sexual relationship, which in the U.S. and societies around the world is typically called marriage.

References:

1. Knight-Ridder News Service, December 10, 1994.

2. W. Masters, V. Johnson, R. Kolodny, *Human Sexuality*, 3rd Edition, Glenview, IL: Scott Foresman & Co., 1988.

3. Green, J., et al, "Detection of human papillomavirus DNA by PCR in semen from patients with and without penile warts," *Genitourinary Medicine*, 67, June, 1991.

4. Ilaria, G., et al, "Detection of HIV-1 DNA Sequences in Pre-ejaculatory Fluid," *The Lancet*, 340, December 12, 1992.

5. Knobel, G.J., "An Urgent Warning - Contraction of HIV Infection During Mutual Masturbation," *South African Medical Journal*, 73, May 21, 1988.

6. Kotwal, G.J., et al, "Detection of Hepatitis C Virus-Specific Antigens in Semen from Non-A, Non-B Hepatitis Patients," *Digestive Diseases and Sciences*, 37:5, May, 1992.

7. van den Brule, A.J.C., et al, "Detection of Chlamydia Trachomatis in Semen of Artificial Insemination Donors by the Polymerase Chain Reaction," *Fertility and Sterility*, 59:5, May, 1993.

8. Bauer, H., et al, "Genital Human Papillomavirus Infection in Female University Students as Determined by a PCR-Based Method," *Journal of the American Medical Association*, 265:4, January 23, 1991.

9. Cone, R.W., et al, "Frequent Detection of Genital Herpes Simplex Virus DNA by Polymerase Chain Reaction on Pregnant Women," *Journal of the American Medical Association*, 272:10, September 14, 1994.

10. *Guidelines for Comprehensive Sexuality Education*, Sex Information and Education Council of the U.S., 1991, p.33.

11. Ibid.

12. *SIECUS Report*, June/July, 1994.

13. Planned Parenthood Federation of America, Inc., *How To Talk To Your Teen About The Facts Of Life*, Revised Version, May, 1993, p.22.

14. Benson, M.D., and Torpy, E.J., "Sexual Behavior in Junior High School Students," *Obstetrics and Gynecology*, 85:2, February, 1995.

4

Abstinence Education Can Prevent Sexually Transmitted Diseases

Kathleen M. Sullivan

Kathleen M. Sullivan is director of Project Reality, an organization that promotes abstinence education.

The opposition to abstinence-only sex education expressed by organizations such as the Sexuality Information and Education Council of the United States (SIECUS) is misguided and self-serving. Giving young people information about condoms and other information about "safe" sex has helped to create an epidemic of teen pregnancy and sexually transmitted diseases (STDs). Children should be taught that abstinence is the only sure way to stay healthy and to prevent STDs.

Amazingly, some people in this country are vigorously discouraging state participation in the new provision for abstinence-education funding contained in the 1996 Welfare Reform Act. They need to understand that abstinence until marriage is not a moral judgment—it is a prescription for physical and emotional health. Those now so determined to silence the abstinence-centered message should open their minds and hearts and welcome this new opportunity to promote the healthiest lifestyle for our children and teens.

A panic cry is now emanating from mixed-message "safe" sex advocates like SIECUS (Sexuality Information and Education Council of the United States), in conjunction with its bureaucratic partners and some in the media, against abstinence education.

They call for "abstaining" from participating in the new opportunity funded by Congress to provide abstinence education. This stance is based on concerns about "survival"—survival of their vast service business that depends on the existence of the problems associated with teens being sexually active rather than the prevention of the sexual activity that causes the problems.

Reprinted from Kathleen M. Sullivan, "Sexual Abstinence: The Healthiest Lifestyle," *St. Louis Post-Dispatch*, June 22, 1997, by permission of the *St. Louis Post-Dispatch*, copyright 1997.

Sexually abstinent healthy adolescents are simply not customers for them.

The results of decades of SIECUS-led so-called "safe" sex condom-centered education show a nation of adolescents suffering from epidemic levels of out-of-wedlock pregnancy and sexually transmitted diseases, all of which are almost entirely preventable by abstaining from sex until marriage. The mixed "safe" sex message has proved to be decidedly "unsafe" for our children.

Eight of the reasons to Say Yes to abstinence education are spelled out in the new law itself. The law defines abstinence education as "an educational or motivational program," that:

- Has as its exclusive purpose teaching the social, psychological and health gains to be realized by abstaining from sexual activity.
- Teaches abstinence from sexual activity outside marriage as the expected standard for all school-age children.
- Teaches that abstinence from sexual activity is the only certain way to avoid out-of-wedlock pregnancy, sexually transmitted diseases and other associated health problems.
- Teaches that a mutually faithful monogamous relationship in the context of marriage is the expected standard of human sexual activity.
- Teaches that sexual activity outside the marriage context is likely to have harmful psychological and physical effects.
- Teaches that bearing children out of wedlock is likely to have harmful consequences for the child, the parents and society.
- Teaches young people how to reject sexual advances and how alcohol and drug use increases vulnerability to sexual advances.
- Teaches the importance of attaining self-sufficiency before engaging in sexual activity.

The vast majority of parents and taxpayers who read those provisions are enthusiastic that public policy is finally reflecting what they know to be a good format for healthy adolescent living.

Abstinence-centered programs work. An abstinence education program administered by Project Reality has been evaluated by Northwestern University Medical School in a study completed in November 1996. The study followed students one year after they had participated in the program. It matched 2,541 students who ranged from 13 to 16 years of age and were evenly split between male and female.

According to the study, 54 percent of the teens who had been recently sexually active before participating in the abstinence-centered education program were no longer recently sexually active one year later. Moreover, one year after this public school classroom instruction, the number of newly sexually active teens surveyed fell 21 percent below the level predicted by their involvement in associated risk behaviors.

Surely, everyone concerned about the health of adolescents should applaud results like these and enthusiastically support the expanded opportunity to offer abstinence education that the funding from Congress affords. Abstinence education has as its only and unassailable goal the promotion of the healthiest lifestyle for our teen-agers.

5

Abstinence-Only Sex Education Is Not Effective in Preventing Sexually Transmitted Diseases

Center for AIDS Prevention Studies

The Center for AIDS Prevention Studies (CAPS), based at the University of California at San Francisco, conducts research and public outreach programs focusing on the prevention of AIDS.

The "abstinence only" approach to sex education—in which students are taught to abstain from sex and all discussion of condoms or safer sex is avoided—is inappropriate for the significant numbers of adolescents who choose to have sex. Sexually active young people need information on how to prevent pregnancies and sexually transmitted diseases (STDs). Religious and political agendas, rather than public health needs, are driving government funding of abstinence education programs whose effectiveness has not been demonstrated in studies. Students should be encouraged to remain abstinent, but they should also be taught comprehensive information about sexuality, including condom usage and other methods of STD prevention.

S chools have become a battleground in the nation's culture wars. In the fight over the hearts, minds—and libidos—of our nation's teenagers, the latest skirmish involves sex education. The question is not whether education about sexuality belongs in the schools (there is well nigh universal accord on this score),[1] but rather, how to approach the topic. "Just say no" is the answer, at least according to a growing number of champions of "abstinence only" curricula. Abstinence-only approaches include discussions of values, character building and refusal skills, while avoiding specific discussions of contraception or safer sex.

Comprehensive sexuality education begins with abstinence but also ac-

Reprinted with permission from "Should We Teach Only Abstinence in Sexuality Education?" HIV Prevention Fact Sheet #30E, published by the Center for AIDS Prevention Studies, University of California, San Francisco, September 1997.

knowledges that many teenagers will choose to have sex and thus need to be aware of the consequences and how to protect themselves. Such programs include instruction in safe sex behavior, including use of condoms and other contraceptives.[2]

The abstinence-only sex education movement has been propelled by the persistent but mistaken belief that comprehensive sexuality education itself somehow seduces teenagers into sexual activity. By this reasoning it follows that schools should either ignore the issue or discuss sexuality only in terms of fear and disease. The casualties in this war are teenagers themselves, denied information about how to prevent pregnancy or sexually transmitted diseases (STDs) in the highly likely event that they have sexual intercourse.

Policy developments

Abstinence-only proponents got a big boost when, as part of the federal welfare reform legislation, Congress earmarked $50 million dollars per year for the next five years [beginning in 1998] for abstinence-only school programs. Eight specific criteria have been established for programs, including the mandate that their "exclusive purpose" be teaching the "social, psychological and health gains" to be realized from abstinence. The block grant requires 75 percent matching funds from other public or private sources, for an annual total of more than $87 million.[3]

Every state in the union applied for the federal abstinence funding. Some expect to use it only for children in early grades or for media campaigns, a strategy which avoids putting a teacher in the position of being unable to answer a question about birth control or barrier methods of protection from high school students.[4]

Abstinence for whom? until when?

Abstinence-only curricula typically seek to encourage abstinence from sexual activity until marriage. In support of this goal, abstinence proponents use arguments that fly in the face of both science and human experience. The federal abstinence provisions include the statement: "Sexual activity outside the context of marriage is likely to have harmful psychological and physical effects." This conclusion is as unsubstantiated as it is startling, in light of the statistic that 93 percent of American men and 80 percent of American women between ages 18 and 59 were not virgins on their wedding night.[4]

In the debate over the role for abstinence in sexuality education, little pain is taken to avoid the distinction, for example, between abstinence for 12- or 13-year-olds versus 17- or 18-year-olds. Few could argue with a near exclusive focus on abstinence for young children. For older teens, sexuality education needs to be relevant for the substantial share of adolescents who choose to have sex. Two thirds (66%) of American high school seniors have had sex.[5]

Pleas to abstain from sex until marriage must also be considered in light of the average age at which Americans first tie the knot (approximately 24 for women and 26 for men).[6] Moreover, the exhortations to avoid sex until marriage have little, if any, meaning for gay teens.

Great expectations?

The sex education debate sometimes grows so heated as to lose a sense of proportion. Great expectations are heaped on school-based programs. Most teaching is assessed by measuring its impact on knowledge rather than behavior outside of the classroom.[7] It is a tall order to establish the relationship between classroom sex education and changes in behaviors such as delays in initiating intercourse or increases in contraceptive use. Classroom instruction must be factored into the conflicting mix of influences from peers, parents, churches and a media barrage of pro-sex messages.

If all young people had safe and secure lives, a "just say no" message by itself might be useful. But for most, risk taking is part of a constellation of internal and external influences. A 1995 national survey reported that 16% of girls whose first intercourse was before age 16 reported that initiation of intercourse was not voluntary.[8] School-based programs by definition also fail to reach many of those at highest risk, such as "runaway" or "throwaway" youth.[9]

Abstinence-only or abstinence plus?

The best sex education begins with abstinence as a starting point, both encouraging it for young people who are not ready for sex and supporting those who choose it for whatever reason. Abstinence-only proponents have criticized more comprehensive approaches for focusing only on "plumbing," sending "mixed messages" and ignoring values. Clearly, the best sex education programs address more than the biology of sex and risk (although kids are owed the basic facts on how their bodies work and how to protect themselves against unintended pregnancy and sexually transmitted diseases).

> *The abstinence-only sex education movement has been propelled by the persistent but mistaken belief that comprehensive sexuality education itself somehow seduces teenagers into sexual activity.*

So far, abstinence-only programs have failed to meet scientific tests of proven effectiveness. A review found only six published studies in the peer-reviewed literature examining abstinence-only programs.[10] None was found effective, in part due to poor evaluation; one was clearly ineffective. If the federal government is going to fund approaches absent any proof of significant program effects, state officials who accept federal dollars should insist that the programs be thoroughly and rigorously evaluated.

The quarter billion dollar federal program for abstinence-only teaching furthers a religious and political, not a public health agenda.[11] Political agendas and discomfort with teen sexuality obstruct the ability to conduct research on which programs work best in preventing HIV and unintended pregnancies. It is not enough to agree on what adults would like young people to hear. Delivery of politically palatable—rather than effective—curricula may serve the interest of adults, but will cheat many young people.

What really works?

For all their antipathy, abstinence-only advocates and comprehensive sexuality education proponents share common goals: the prevention of unintended pregnancies, HIV and other STDs. A number of comprehensive sex education curricula examined in rigorous studies have achieved modest delays in sexual intercourse, reductions in number of partners, and increases in contraceptive use. A national review outlined a variety of elements of effective programs: tailoring to the age and experience of the audience; focus on risky sexual behavior; sound theoretical foundation; provision of basic facts about avoiding risks of unprotected sex; acknowledgement of social pressures to have sex; and practice in communication, negotiation and refusal skills.[10]

Abstinence-only programs have failed to meet scientific tests of proven effectiveness.

The guardians of quality education, including teachers, parents, school boards, and legislators have a duty to consider more than the leanings of one advocacy group or another. Credible, objective evidence about the ability of specific programs to achieve their goals is essential. Decision makers need to separate value questions from questions of effectiveness in sex education, and find the common ground.

Says who?

1. Kaiser Family Foundation. *The Kaiser Survey on Americans and AIDS/HIV.* Menlo Park, CA: 1998.

2. National Institutes of Health. *Interventions to Prevent HIV Risk Behaviors. Consensus Development Conference Statement.* Washington, DC: 1997; Feb. 11–13.

3. Block Grant Guidance for the Abstinence Education Provision of the 1996 Welfare Law P.L. 104-193. For more information, contact: Department of Health and Human Services, PHS/HRSA/MCHB/OD/CB-18-20, 5600 Fishers Lane, Rockville, MD 20857, (301) 443-0205.

4. Associated Press. Sex education that teaches abstinence wins support. *New York Times.* July 23, 1997; A19.

5. Centers for Disease Control and Prevention. Youth risk behavior surveillance-United States, 1995. *Morbidity and Mortality Weekly Report.* 1996; 45 (No. SS-4): 1–86.

6. The Alan Guttmacher Institute. *Sex and America's Teenagers.* New York, 1994. http://www.agi-usa.org/

7. Kirby D. Sex and HIV/AIDS education in schools. *British Medical Journal.* 1995; 311:403.

8. National Center for Health Statistics. National Survey of Family Growth, cycle IV: 1990 telephone reinterview. Hyattsville, MD: US Department of Health and Human Services; 1995.

9. Rotheram-Borus M.J., Koopman C., Haignere C., et al. Reducing HIV risk

behaviors among runaway adolescents. *Journal of the American Medical Association.* 1991; 266: 1237–1241.

10. Kirby D. *No Easy Answers: Research Findings on Programs to Reduce Teen Pregnancy.* Washington, DC: National Campaign to Prevent Teen Pregnancy; 1997.

11. Ehrhardt A.A. Our view of adolescent sexuality—a focus on risk behavior without the developmental context. *American Journal of Public Health.* 1996; 86: 1523–1525.

6

Teenagers Should Be Taught About and Provided with Condoms

M. Joycelyn Elders

M. Joycelyn Elders, U.S. Surgeon General from 1993 to 1994, is a pediatric endocrinologist and author.

America's children are being placed at risk for AIDS and other sexually transmitted diseases (STDs) because parents and teachers are reluctant to discuss the use of condoms. Promoting abstinence as the only means of STD prevention is not appropriate for all youth, many of whom reach puberty—and become aware of sexual feelings—at a relatively young age. Classroom abstinence education is also of little use to teen females who are sexually abused by older men. The United States must follow the example of other nations and provide young people with both comprehensive sex education and condoms to protect them from STDs.

These days we confuse ignorance with innocence. Many adults believe (wrongly) that children are asexual, have no sexual thoughts, feelings or desires and shouldn't become aware of sex in any way before puberty. But in fact, sexual expression is coming earlier to teens, not because of loose morals or lack of values, but because children reach menses and puberty at an increasingly younger age. Yet by leaving them in the lurch rather than helping them understand the changes in their bodies, we punish our youth for what is literally beyond their control.

Few children today receive accurate, comprehensive health education at home; their mostly uninformed and anxious parents can't offer it. However, almost all children go to school, and it is there that they could most likely be prepared for a sexually healthy life. For we are losing our children and youth to disease, and it is time to act.

Consider these global statistics: In 1996, 1.5 million people, including 350,000 children and youth, died of AIDS. Of the 30 million people infected with HIV, 2.6 million—nearly one in 10—are adolescent or

Reprinted from M. Joycelyn Elders, "Respect Your Elders!" *POZ*, December 1997, © POZ Publishing L.L.C., with permission. For *POZ* subscriptions, call 800-973-2376.

younger. Most new infections occur in people under 25, and about 80 percent of all adult infections occur through unprotected sexual intercourse—yet *condom* is still a naughty word in the United States.

Abstinence has been widely endorsed and heavily financed by the federal government. The Sexuality Information and Education Council of the United States (SIECUS) reported that all 50 states filed applications for their share of $50 million in federal funds for the 1996 welfare reform bill's abstinence-only education program. So while we refuse to support sexuality education, we try to legislate morals. But abstinence is a highly risky philosophy in which to put our entire trust. In his book *Solving America's Sexual Crises,* sociologist Ira Reiss puts it best when he writes, "Vows of abstinence break more easily than do condoms."

Preventing new infections in the United States by promoting abstinence alone may never be accomplished, since three-quarters of all teen pregnancies are fathered by adult males. A recent study reveals a related— and very disturbing—trend: More adolescent girls than boys are diagnosed with HIV. According to the Centers for Disease Control and Prevention (CDC), 90 percent of the AIDS cases under age 20 are among girls. And these infections are generally not getting HIV from teen-age boys. In fact, many of the men responsible for infecting them are relatives.

It has been estimated that one in three girls is sexually abused by age 18, and one in four by age 14. These preteens—who cannot "just say no"—likely feel a special sense of shame and despair when their teachers emphasize that the only appropriate method for birth control and disease prevention is abstinence. Let's face it: Teen-agers are having sex, and they need condoms.

In 1997, Shari Lo, a California sophomore, won a trophy at her high school science fair for a project measuring condom reliability. She was on her way to the regional science-fair competition when the school superintendent disqualified her project, explaining that "because it is on condom reliability, it encourages safe sex. Our philosophy is abstinence, not safe sex."

We are losing our children and youth to disease, and it is time to act.

It's true—albeit rarely stated so bluntly—that as a nation, we care more about philosophy than the lives of our youth. That's why U.S. teens have the highest rates of pregnancy, childbirth, abortion and HIV in the developed world—even though adolescent sexual activity and the age of initial sexual contact in other countries is similar to ours. Adolescents in countries such as Sweden, the Netherlands, Britain and France have much lower rates of sexually transmitted diseases (STDs) and HIV than our own. Why? For one thing, all other developed nations have comprehensive health and sexuality education from kindergarten to grade 12. Discussion of contraception—including condoms—is widespread in the media, and universal health care makes birth control available and affordable. Finland's government sends out a brochure to every 16-year-old on his or her birthday that presents a positive depiction of adolescent sexuality, talks about responsibility and comes with a latex condom.

While our young are dying, we are quibbling over methods. Nationwide, one million teenage girls became pregnant in 1996, and half that number gave birth; three million youths got STDs. HIV infections and AIDS cases are both increasing fastest among adolescents.

Let's face it: Teen-agers are having sex, and they need condoms.

Abstinence works for many of our youth. However, I'm not willing to just throw away all the rest for whom it does not work for one reason or another. We are at a low point in our nation's history in terms of caring for our children. We've tried legislating morals, and that didn't work. We've tried just saying no, and that didn't work. We've tried ignorance, and that didn't work. Why don't we try education? Let's end this shameful era by standing up and stepping out to save our precious children.

7

Condoms Do Not Protect Teenagers from Sexually Transmitted Diseases

John D. Hartigan

John D. Hartigan is a corporate lawyer who has done volunteer legal work in the fields of public health and public education.

Studies have shown that school-based condom distribution programs have failed to achieve their goals of protecting youth from HIV infection and other sexually transmitted diseases and preventing teen pregnancies. Young people lack the necessary discipline to use condoms carefully and correctly. In addition, supplying teenagers with condoms encourages greater sexual activity. Educators must find another approach to protect America's young people from sexually transmitted diseases.

The theory generally advanced to justify distributing condoms to teenagers is that this will protect them against pregnancy and HIV infection if they choose to be sexually active. However, study after study shows that this policy just doesn't work in practice. In real life, handing out condoms to teenagers is a prescription for disaster.

The main reason for this is that teenagers are simply too impulsive and undisciplined to use condoms with the rigorous care needed to avoid failure. A 1988 survey conducted in the United States revealed that more than 27 percent of all never-married, low-income teenage girls who depend on condoms for birth control become pregnant in their first year of condom use.[1]

To make matters worse, supplying teenagers with condoms inevitably produces a marked increase in their sexual activity. For example, when San Francisco's Balboa High School started giving students coupons that they could exchange for condoms at a nearby city dispensary, the percentage of female students engaging in sexual intercourse jumped by one-fourth in just two years.[2] Similarly, a study of adolescents taking part in a three-year condom promotion experiment in Switzerland showed that

Reprinted from John Hartigan, "The Disastrous Results of Condom Distribution Programs," *In Focus*, November 1997, by permission of the Family Research Council.

the proportion of girls under the age of 17 engaging in sexual activity increased by almost two-thirds—from 36 to 57 percent.[3]

Three studies

Given these inherent drawbacks, it is hardly surprising that school-based and school-linked condom dispensation programs never succeed. Instead of reducing pregnancies, they almost always do just the opposite. To illustrate, consider the outcomes of three highly revealing studies conducted in major U.S. cities:
 • San Francisco—Even though students were exposed to "graphic demonstrations" of proper condom use,[4] the Balboa High School condom availability program turned out to be a colossal failure. The percentage of sexually active students using condoms almost doubled,[5] but, despite that supposedly positive change in student sexual behavior, the school's overall pregnancy rate increased by one-fourth.[6] With an increase in pregnancy, it can be assumed that there was a similar increase in student exposure to HIV infection and other sexually-transmitted diseases.
 • St. Paul and Dallas—In two school-based programs that dispensed condoms rather than coupons, the results were even worse than those in San Francisco. Specifically, a St. Paul program that was supposed to reduce annual teenage births actually caused them to spiral upward by one-third (from 22 per 1,000 to 29 per 1,000).[7] An inner-city Dallas school that distributed condoms ended up with an 11.2 percent overall pregnancy rate, 47 percent higher than the 7.6 percent overall pregnancy rate found in an almost identical Dallas school that did not implement such a program.[8]

The limits of expert counseling

Moreover, it is folly to believe that dispensing condoms to teenagers might work better if accompanied by expert counseling on how to use condoms without mishap. As the following summary [see box on next page] indicates, efforts to bring about effective condom use through intensive counseling have proved uniformly unsuccessful, even when the persons being counseled are adult females who are very strongly motivated to avoid pregnancy and HIV infection.

Given this long record of failure, the time has come for educators and health officials to abandon their blind faith in condoms and face the fact that supplying youngsters with condoms does not reduce teenage pregnancies or HIV infections. On the contrary, all the available evidence shows that condom distribution will only worsen the consequences of teenagers' sexual activity. Clearly, another approach needs to be taken if our young people are going to be protected from the scourges of teen pregnancy, sexually-transmitted diseases, and HIV.

Notes

   1. Elise F. Jones and Jacqueline D. Forrest, "Contraceptive Failure Rates Based on the 1988 NSFG," *Family Planning Perspectives*, January/February 1992, pp. 12–19. See Table 2, p. 15.

2. Douglas Kirby, *et al.*, *An Assessment of Six School-Based Clinics: Services, Impact and Potential* (Center for Population Options, 1989), pp. 32, 65; and "Six School-Based Clinics: Their Reproductive Health Services and Impact on Sexual Behavior," *Family Planning Perspectives*, January/February 1991, pp. 6–16, at pp. 11–12. For brevity, the earlier of these Kirby studies is hereafter cited as the "1989 Report" and the more recent as the "1991 Report."

3. Dominique Hausser and P.A. Michaud, "Does a Condom-Promoting Strategy (the Swiss STOP-AIDS Campaign) Modify Sexual Behavior Among Adolescents?" *Pediatrics*, April 1994, Table 3, p. 582.

4. 1989 Report, p. 65.

5. 1989 Report, p. 64.

6. Before the condom coupon experiment began, 37 percent of the school's female students were sexually active, and the annual pregnancy rate was 5.9 percent per year (i.e., 37% x 16%). When the experiment ended two years later, 46 percent of the school's female students were sexually active, and the annual pregnancy rate among these girls was 16 percent, so the school's overall pregnancy rate was 7.4 percent per year (i.e., 46% x 16%, or one-fourth higher than when the experiment started). See 1991 Report, Table 3, p. 11, and Table 8, p. 15.

7. Douglas Kirby, *et al.*, "The Effects of School-Based Health Clinics in St.

Women Receiving Counseling	Outcome
68 mainly black and Hispanic U.S. women aged 18 to 65 with stable sex partners	7.9 percent of condoms slipped off during intercourse or broke during intercourse or withdrawal. Of the remaining condoms, 7.2 percent slipped off during withdrawal.[9]
18 uninfected adult Florida women with HIV-positive sex partners	Three of the women (16 percent of the cohort) became HIV-infected within 18 months.[10]
31 uninfected adult French women with HIV-positive sex partners	17 of these women "did not adhere to the use of condoms," and three of them were infected.[11]
404 uninfected adult European women with HIV-positive sex partners	Only 49 of these women used condoms all or most of the time, and six of those 49 were infected.[12]
163 uninfected adult European women with HIV-positive sex partners	74 of these women failed to use condoms consistently, and eight of these 74 were infected.[13]

Paul on School-Wide Birthrates," *Family Planning Perspectives*, January/February 1993, pp. 12–16. See Table 2, p. 15.

8. At the end of the two-year experiment, 80 percent of the girls in the school that dispensed condoms were sexually active, and the annual pregnancy rate was 11.2 percent per year (i.e., 80% x 14%). By contrast, only 76 percent of the girls in the school that did not dispense condoms had ever engaged in sex, and the annual pregnancy rate among these girls was only 10 percent, so the school's overall pregnancy rate was only 7.6 percent per year (i.e., 76% x 10%). Thus, the overall pregnancy rate in the school that dispensed condoms was 1.47 times the overall pregnancy rate in the otherwise identical sister school that did not dispense condoms. See 1991 Report, Table 3, p. 11, and Table 8, p. 15.

9. James Trussell, *et al.*, "Condom Slippage and Breakage Rates," *Family Planning Perspectives*, January/February 1992, pp. 20–23. See p. 20 and Table 1, p. 22.

10. Margaret Fischl, *et al.*, "Heterosexual Transmission of Human Immuno-deficiency Virus (HIV): Relationship of Sexual Practices to Seroconversion," Third International Conference on AIDS, June 1987, *Abstracts Volume*, p. 178.

11. Y. Laurian, *et al.*, "HIV Infection in Sexual Partners of HIV-Seropositive Patients With Hemophilia," *New England Journal of Medicine*, January 19, 1989, p. 183.

12. European Study Group on Heterosexual Transmission of HIV, "Comparison of female to male and male to female transmission of HIV in stable couples," *British Medical Journal*, March 28, 1992, pp. 809–813. See Table 1, p. 810.

13. Isabelle de Vicenzi, *et al.*, "A Longitudinal Study of Human Immunodeficiency Virus Transmission by Heterosexual Partners," *New England Journal of Medicine*, August 11, 1994, pp. 341–346. See p. 343.

8

Bias and Discrimination Against Women Impede Efforts to Prevent Sexually Transmitted Diseases

Hilary Hinds Kitasei

Hilary Hinds Kitasei is a freelance writer who reports frequently on health issues.

The American public health approach to sexually transmitted diseases (STDs) is based on the outmoded assumption that men are the primary victims. But STDs are also a serious health problem for women. Women are at a higher risk than men for being infected in any single sexual encounter and are more likely than men to suffer long-term complications. Many cases of STDs among women go undiagnosed and untreated because the women show no immediate symptoms and because doctors fail to detect their condition. Public funding for STD treatment and prevention must be increased and targeted toward women, and doctors and patients must be educated about the need for regular STD testing for sexually active women.

When the doors of the public clinic for sexually transmitted diseases (STDs) in southeast Washington, D.C., open at 8:00 in the morning, a throng of men and a few women are waiting outside. Often they are there because painful symptoms have alerted them to the fact that they may have a sexually transmitted infection. Because the clinic sees a limited number of patients, those who arrive early enough will be treated; the rest will go away, unseen and still infected.

Meanwhile, at a private gynecologist's office nearby, a woman has a routine exam. The doctor questions her about her choice of contraceptive, but does not ask for—nor does the patient offer—information about her sex life. Since she has no obvious symptoms, both she and her doctor assume she does not have an STD.

The people standing in line at that clinic have a better chance of being treated for their STDs. Even if they have to come back another day, they at least know they may be infected. But if you're a woman who has contracted an STD and has no telltale signs of infection, as is often true, you risk not receiving treatment until the disease is so far along that severe complications are almost inevitable.

An epidemic

The U.S. is in the midst of an epidemic of STDs, which include bacterial diseases such as syphilis, gonorrhea, and chlamydia and viral infections such as herpes and human papillomavirus (HPV), as well as human immunodeficiency virus (HIV). It is an epidemic that disproportionately affects women. On average, says Mead Over, a health economist at the World Bank, "women get infected at a younger age than men and they remain infectious longer—nearly three times as long in cases of gonorrhea and chlamydia—and are only half as likely to have any detectable symptoms." A woman is also twice as likely as a man to acquire an infection in any single encounter. Women are often asymptomatic because the female reproductive tract provides internal cover for the majority of symptoms, making them harder to detect. In 75 percent of chlamydia cases among women, for example, there are no obvious signs of disease.

Lacking symptoms, most women are neither tested for STDs nor treated, and so are more likely than men to suffer serious long-term complications such as infertility. They also risk passing an infection to a child during birth. Teenage girls are at an even greater risk than adults. An adolescent's cervix is more susceptible to infections of the lower reproductive tract, such as chlamydia. In addition, because teenagers have a higher rate of reinfection, they are more likely to experience long-term complications like infertility and ectopic pregnancy. Annually, three million teenagers contract STDs, and teenage girls have the highest rate of hospitalization in the U.S. for pelvic inflammatory disease (PID) caused by untreated chlamydia or gonorrhea.

Lacking symptoms, most women are neither tested for STDs nor treated.

Whether bacterial or viral, all STDs increase the risk of acquiring HIV upon exposure. One obvious reason is that a genital lesion enables HIV to enter the bloodstream during sexual activity. STDs may also weaken the immune system, thus increasing the likelihood of infection if a person is exposed to HIV. The link between chlamydia and HIV is one that health experts are watching carefully. "If we could control chlamydia, we could potentially reduce the incidence of new cases of HIV in women by as much as 40 percent," Kathleen Tooney, a former U.S. special assistant for STD prevention at the Centers for Disease Control (CDC), has said. The greater vulnerability of women to all STDs, including HIV, is one of the reasons that AIDS is increasing faster among women than men.

A misguided public health approach

How did we get here? In the U.S., we have a public health approach to STDs in which the people most susceptible are the least informed and the least studied. The reasons for the epidemic are directly related to an outmoded system that still assumes that men are the primary victims of STDs and that diseases prevalent 50 years ago are the ones to watch. As a result, at least 75 percent of government funding goes to treating and tracking syphilis and gonorrhea, although they account for fewer than 10 percent of new STD cases reported each year. Meanwhile, chlamydia, which represents a third of all reported bacterial STD cases—some four million a year—and is the most prevalent STD in the U.S., gets 10 percent.

This public health approach to STDs was developed during the 1940s, when soldiers posted at military bases were warned about "loose women" who "carried" disease. It was assumed that "good women" were not infected with sexually transmitted diseases and therefore did not need to be checked. This approach, which results in the mass screening and treatment of men, is designed to protect men's health and women's "reputations." When it comes to women and STDs, U.S. public health policy might best be classified as "don't ask, don't tell."

The reasons for the epidemic are directly related to an outmoded system that still assumes that men are the primary victims of STDs.

This translates into some scary scenarios: newly virulent strains of gonorrhea are cropping up that have developed resistance to some of the antibiotics normally used. Even syphilis, which can be cured with penicillin, has been at record levels in recent years, mostly because money for public health screenings has dried up. But the rise of sexually transmitted viruses is of even greater concern, since these are incurable. For example, the CDC estimates that 31 million people in the U.S. have genital herpes.

The public health system is unable to cope with STDs because it is locked into detection methods that miss the target, both in terms of those who are at risk and the diseases that are most prevalent. Take chlamydia: both the disease and the young girls who are most likely to get it are off the public health system's radar. Government money goes to STD clinics that track diseases among poor, inner-city males. But women rarely go to those clinics: the long wait and the focus on men keep them away. If they discover that they have chlamydia, it is usually through gynecological checkups where a health care provider detects signs of the disease. Most young and low-income women receive gynecological care at family planning clinics, but these clinics get only a very small portion of state and federal funds designated for STD control. The fact that family planning clinics get any money at all is primarily because women health activists have pushed for it by stressing the link between STDs and infertility.

Another problem is that chlamydia and a host of other STDs are simply not being tracked systematically. Syphilis and gonorrhea are the only ones (other than HIV) that doctors and clinics must report to the CDC. Many health care providers don't feel they have to test for other diseases unless symptoms are present—leaving large numbers of infected women untreated.

The system also relies on an outdated notion of where the majority of STDs occur. Most public clinics are in inner cities, where syphilis and gonorrhea are most prevalent—thus the focus on those two as the only "reportable" STDs. But as is true for all STDs, neither race nor income level nor geography is the most important risk factor. Behavior is. Failing to follow safer sex practices and having multiple partners are the two things that increase the likelihood of a woman getting an STD. But because of classist and racist stereotypes, the people being tracked are not necessarily the ones most at risk. For example, too many studies assume that African American women have the highest number of partners and are therefore most susceptible to STDs. But although African American women are less likely to be married than European American women, and therefore may have several partners over a lifetime, the fact is that single white female college graduates have more sex partners than any other female group. Nevertheless, they are rarely tested, their rates of infection rarely show up in statistics, and their risk is greatly underrepresented in public health reporting.

The way this skews reality can be seen in a new CDC study that compared data from a survey of women who were asked if they had ever had gonorrhea to the cases reported by public health clinics and private doctors. The majority (55 percent) of women who reported that they had ever had gonorrhea were white, but white women account for only 19 percent of the annual cases reported by clinics and doctors. Only 31.9 percent of black women reported having had gonorrhea, but they made up fully three quarters (76.9 percent) of the cases reported by doctors and clinics. Latinas constituted 9.2 percent of the self-reported cases, whereas the government data showed only 3.1 percent.

Every sexually active woman must demand that her clinic or doctor test her.

These oversights on the part of doctors and clinics can be devastating. This is especially true when it comes to viral STDs—there are no cures, but the symptoms can be mitigated. Human papillomavirus (HPV), for example, has emerged as a virus of great concern, because of both its prevalence and a growing apprehension that certain strains are powerfully linked to cervical cancer. Up to 19 percent of women college students seeking routine gynecological care at their university health services have been found to be carrying one of the HPV strains linked to cervical cancer, yet in a 1994 survey of primary care physicians, only 31 percent asked patients about condom use and 22 percent asked about the number of sex partners—but 94 percent asked about smoking cigarettes.

Controlling the epidemic

If the epidemic of STDs is to be controlled, public funding for education, detection, and treatment will have to increase—no easy task during an era of spending cutbacks. STD spending is 23 percent less in real dollars than it was in 1950, when the U.S. was waging an all-out campaign to eradicate syphilis. The front line of the government's program continues to be public clinics serving walk-in patients with obvious symptoms. Family planning clinics, which deliver most STD services to women, receive almost no funding for this effort and end up spending money meant to provide birth control options.

While there is a need to continue providing STD services in areas where little or no other health care is available, there is also a need to reach many more communities, particularly with education campaigns. The same CDC study that documented the difference between actual cases of gonorrhea and reports of it indicated that knowledge of STDs is key to knowing what to do about them. Chlamydia, the most common STD, was less well known and the least reported in that study. Health professionals must also rethink what they are telling young women. In an effort to prevent teenage pregnancy, hormonal contraceptives—such as the Pill or Norplant—are being pushed, but they fail to protect against STDs.

In order to reach all women at risk, including lesbians, older women, and adolescents, sexual health has to be separated from reproductive health. Doctors and patients must be educated about the need for regular testing for STDs. That means that every sexually active woman must demand that her clinic or doctor test her. Doctors and patients must also dump old notions of who is at risk. Too many of us are.

"Don't ask, don't tell" has amounted to a policy that endangers the lives of women.

9

Concerns About Civil Rights Have Hobbled Efforts to Control AIDS

Chandler Burr

Chandler Burr is a journalist and contributing editor to U.S. News & World Report. *He is the author of the book* A Separate Creation: The Search for the Biological Origins of Sexual Orientation.

Traditional public health measures—which include routine testing for disease, reporting the names of those infected to public health authorities, and tracing and notifying people who may have been exposed to the disease—could have saved thousands of lives if used against AIDS. However, U.S. public health officials did not take such actions because they feared violating people's rights to privacy and freedom from discrimination and because gay organizations strongly opposed these measures. A comparison of the United States with Cuba—a country that did follow standard epidemiological measures—reveals how badly the United States has failed in controlling the AIDS epidemic.

Dr. Tom Coburn, a low-key 50-year-old family GP who practices obstetrics, mostly for Medicaid patients, in Muskogee, Oklahoma, is the front-runner for the title of Gay Activists' Public Enemy Number One. It is a designation he is happy to contend for.

In his other job as a Republican congressman ("not my *profession*, I'm a doctor"), Coburn is the author and primary sponsor of HR-1062, The AIDS Prevention Act of 1997. All the major liberal, civil-liberties, gay, and AIDS organizations—the American Civil Liberties Union (ACLU), the Gay and Lesbian Medical Association, National Organization for Women (NOW), the AIDS Action Council, Gay Men's Health Crisis, People for the American Way, and so on—are in full assault mode against the bill, which if enacted would do something to the AIDS epidemic we've never done before: apply to it the standard public-health disease-containment measures of routine testing of at-risk individuals (although individuals should have the right to refuse testing), confidential reporting by name of those infected to local health authorities, and aggressive partner notification. In other words, it will make public-health personnel treat AIDS—the number one killer of Americans aged 25 to 44—like any other infectious disease.

AIDS, in partial fulfillment of its own championship in the annals of epidemiology (winner, "Most Politicized Disease in the History of the Whole World"), has never been attacked with these measures. Why? Because of a judgment call about who would get hurt. When AIDS weighed in in full force in the mid 1980s, the gay community decided that the disease hurt homosexuals vulnerable to a hostile society at least as much by pitilessly outing them as it did by killing them. Standard public health is about identifying the infected in order to prevent further transmission, but with AIDS, identification was the problem. The gay community, with the best of intentions, believed that the messy, complex, often desperate job of protecting the public health against contagion could be made nice and not hurt anyone.

This decision produced a rather astounding display of political power. After intense lobbying on the part of gay organizations, state and local public-health officials ultimately with the avid support of the mighty Centers for Disease Control (CDC), made AIDS the first epidemic treated as a civil-rights issue and a threat to individual privacy. All sorts of violations were presented: people with AIDS being expelled from their homes, losing their jobs, being dropped by their insurers. But the greatest threat was that the government would use the virus as an excuse to conduct a new holocaust. This was an explicit and constant warning by the gay and civil-liberties organizations—and they told us there was a country that actually did it: Cuba. Cuba set up concentration camps. Juanita Darling in the *Los Angeles Times* of July 24, 1997, recounted in (relatively) moderate tone what these organizations have been saying for years: "Cuba has been notorious for its draconian treatment of people infected with the virus that causes AIDS: The government has rounded up everyone infected with the human immunodeficiency virus and locked them in sanitariums until they developed AIDS and died." The Cubans, we were told, used traditional epidemiology—testing, reporting, and notification—to track down and persecute homosexuals, and were we to use these measures in the U.S., they would surely be deployed in the same way. So we did not.

After intense lobbying on the part of gay organizations, state and local public-health officials . . . made AIDS the first epidemic treated as a civil-rights issue.

What we did instead was use sex education, condoms, and needle exchange, essentially asking people to learn how HIV is transmitted and then to be careful. Columbia University's Ron Bayer created a name for this brand new civil-rights-centered public health—"AIDS exceptionalism"—and in the U.S. all efforts to combat this epidemic have thus been made to pass a high-minded-sounding test: they must not hurt the civil liberties or personal fortunes of the infected. The practice of epidemiology, created by John Snow in the London cholera epidemic of the mid

1880s and used since then to combat tuberculosis, polio, syphilis and gonorrhea, influenza, and on and on, has in the case of AIDS been fundamentally altered.

Rep. Coburn with his bill is demanding a re-examination of the way our country has responded to this public-health crisis. He is doing this in a forward-looking way: HR-1062 aims to get AIDS treated from now on like other diseases from TB to hepatitis A. [Congress had not voted on HR-1062 as of July 1998.] But what makes HR-1062 so controversial is its retrospective aspect. It calls the past silently but inescapably into question.

Serious accusations

At 9:00 A.M. on March 13, 1997, at the press conference introducing the bill, Rep. Coburn stepped up to the lectern in the Rayburn House Office Building, looked at the reporters (in the seats), his allies (behind him), and AIDS organizations' spokesmen (grimly lining the walls like prison guards anticipating a riot), and began, "I am convinced that a hundred thousand deaths could have been averted if we had adopted these basic public-health measures in the first place." Expand this statement and it reads: Tom Coburn believes that at least a hundred thousand people, mostly gay men, who should be alive today are dead because certain people, again mostly gay men, with the best of intentions, used their political power to suspend disease-control measures for AIDS.

This is why HR-1062 is, although Coburn has never put it this way, much more than just another bill: it is an accusation. It is the epidemiological equivalent of a class-action lawsuit, an assertion that gay leaders, abetted by their liberal allies, committed mass manslaughter by instituting policies which ensured that in this medical conflagration a virus would use their own people as kindling.

Coburn's is an observation increasingly echoed by the medical establishment. On a national radio show a few weeks after Coburn's press conference, Dr. Frank Judson of Denver's Public Health Department stated: "I have no doubt that lots of people have become infected and lost their lives as a result of these irrational policies we've chosen to follow." Which lends credence to statements of Rep. Coburn's such as: "Public health works, and the people who have died of this disease should have been provided it."

But wait. There's more. Arguably worse than slaughtering your own is slaughtering others. The rate at which people are becoming infected with AIDS is thought to be slowing down only within one demographic group: gay men. Coburn points out that it is growing, at a rather astounding rate, among blacks, Hispanics, and women, most especially women who have sexual relations with intravenous drug users. If Dr. Coburn is correct in saying that "the new public health" took gay lives, then gay men demanding that these same policies be applied to others at-risk is both breathtakingly nearsighted and breathtakingly irresponsible. The political repercussions are chilling. What, to take a for-instance, would happen if the black community were to decide one day that traditional epidemiology would have prevented the transmission of HIV to tens if not hundreds of thousands of black people? Or that the problem of skyrocketing rates of HIV infection among blacks could have been averted but was not owing to gays' blind, dogmatic adherence to self-interest?

Dr. Coburn's accusation is only as solid as the data on which it rests. And here is where things get odd. There are, in fact, excellent data. They come from a country which has bent over backward to care for its citizens infected with HIV, probably spending more on AIDS in proportion to its GNP than any other nation. It has also instituted a traditional epidemiological regimen against AIDS. It has the most successful AIDS-containment policy of any country in the world. The country is the same one accused of carrying out a holocaust against AIDS sufferers: Cuba.

AIDS policies in Cuba

The first AIDS case in Cuba surfaced in 1985. If AIDS began as a gay disease in the United States, in Cuba it first turned up in heterosexual soldiers back from their country's military exploits in Africa; that 1985 case was a soldier returning from Mozambique. In Africa, anal intercourse, the most efficient way of spreading the virus, is a quite common means of preserving technical virginity in girls. The rate of sexually transmitted diseases (STDs), which also greatly facilitate transmission, is also extremely high. The sanatariums, in Cuba, were built by the army for the country's returning heroes; persecution of homosexuals had nothing to do with it. In fact, when the disease spread to homosexuals, the sanitariums were among the few places where gay couples were allowed to live together openly. Furthermore, the sanitariums provided and provide the best medical care available in Cuba, 3,500 calories a day, and AIDS-prevention information, not to mention ice cream and air conditioning. Since around 1989, AIDS sufferers have in general been able to choose whether to stay in a sanitarium or live at home, and it has often been difficult to get people to leave.

In any case, as tools for combatting AIDS, the sanitariums are of secondary importance. The real story is the public-health policy Cuba put in place. And this was fiercely and completely traditional. Dr. Jorge Perez, the head of the Pedro Kouri Institute for Tropical and Infectious Diseases and the architect of Cuba's anti-AIDS plan, told me recently in Havana, "From the beginning we treated AIDS like an STD." This meant testing, reporting, and partner notification. "I as a doctor don't have to have someone's permission to test them," said Perez. "I don't ask. Testing isn't mandatory, but I simply prescribe a test when I have good reason." In most of the United States, this is illegal when the test is for HIV.

> *[Cuba] has the most successful AIDS-containment policy of any country in the world.*

"We have a very active screening program," said Dr. Rigoberto Torres, "testing risk groups, pregnant women, inmates." Again, these practices, which are standard public-health procedures, have been almost entirely blocked in the U.S. by ACLU lawsuits and AIDS political activism, as has contact tracing, which is acknowledged as the most efficient, cost-effective way of identifying infections in subgroups of populations. Studies in the U.S. have shown that partner notification finds more infected people then any other method, and it finds them earlier, when their T-cell count is higher and their prognosis is better.

For the most part, however, we Americans don't notify, or we don't notify effectively, simply because it might "invade people's privacy"—a privacy that has already been invaded by a deadly although treatable virus. Of testing, reporting, and notification Perez says, "These three things are the key of the Cuban [traditionalist] program. We have now done 2 million tests in a population of 11 million, and virtually all sexually active people have been tested. The main source of infected people we get is through contact tracing, about 50 to 60 per cent."

Cuba's results

The results of Cuba's program speak for themselves. In 1997, 45,000 people out of the 260-million American population will become infected with the AIDS virus, and so far over 362,000 Americans have died; Cuba, with an 11-million population, has since the start of the epidemic seen 1,681 infected. So far, 442 have died. Control for the population difference, and here is what you get: There have been 35 times more AIDS deaths per capita in the United States than in Cuba. (Of all Americans alive since the start of the epidemic, AIDS has killed 0.14 per cent of them; in Cuba, it has killed 0.004 per cent.)

Compare Cuba to New York City, with its population of around 7.5 million: An estimated 128,700 New Yorkers live with AIDS or HIV, and 63,789 have died. Is very urban New York an unfair comparison? Take Ohio, a Midwestern, predominantly rural state with a population almost exactly the same size as Cuba's: an estimated 10,000 to 18,000 people are HIV positive (this is only an estimate because Ohio doesn't permit HIV reporting), and there have been 9,238 cases of AIDS. Illinois, also Cuba's size, estimates that 30,000 of its citizens are in 1997 HIV-infected (Cuba: 1,239). It has had 19,507 AIDS cases (Cuba: 1,681) and counting.

Look at it another way: In 1993 (the last year for which there are figures) the World Health Organization reported that the U.S. had 276 annual new cases of AIDS per million people. Puerto Rico, another Caribbean island but with one-third Cuba's population, had 654. Brazil was at 75.4, Mexico at 46, and Argentina at 48 per million.

Cuba was at 7. And Cuba's pediatric AIDS system cares for a total of 5 children, whereas Pennsylvania, with the same population, has 122. In the U.S. in 1996, there were 678 pediatric AIDS cases reported to the CDC, which means that our per-capita figure for children with AIDS is 6.5 times higher than Cuba's.

The figures are neither a statistical trick nor Castroite propaganda. (Fidel Castro had nothing to do with Cuba's AIDS program, by the way; it is people like Perez, Torres, and Manuel Santine, Cuba's chief epidemiologist, who created and run it.) Cuba's health-care standards are approximately equal to ours; its infant-mortality rate, a good overall indicator, is 11 deaths per 1,000 live births, near the 7 figure of the U.S., UK, and France. (Canada's is 6. The Dominican Republic's and Mexico's are 35 and 34 respectively.) And one epidemiologist told me of the AIDS stats: "Cuban figures are absolutely reliable and dependable. Surveillance is quite good because they have essentially universal testing and an excellent tracking system. We trust the Cuban figures more than any other country's, where there is underreporting and misdiagnosis, but, um, don't quote me on that." He meant the United States; the CDC will tell you there could be anywhere from 650,000 to 900,000 Americans infected with HIV; it is the lack of traditional testing that prevents the compilation of a more accurate figure. In Cuba, meanwhile, there are reportedly 1,239 people living with HIV, and the number is probably quite close to exact. If we take the CDC's upper figure (the estimates of some experts are higher) and put it on a per-capita basis, there are around 31 times more HIV-positive Americans than Cubans.

Besides demonstrating the success traditional methods have against AIDS, the Cuban example also challenges our strategy of throwing condoms at the problem. One American working on AIDS in Cuba told me he had seen "extraordinarily low condom use." Although some condoms of Dutch manufacture are now available, Cuba for years imported Chinese condoms, which were of notoriously low quality—they were actually used by Cubans not in bed but at the market as chits to buy sugar—and yet the infection rate is still dramatically lower than America's. This shouldn't be the case if condoms are the answer and if old-fashioned public health doesn't work.

There have been 35 times more AIDS deaths per capita in the United States than in Cuba.

This is not to say that the Cuban model *per se* would be right for the United States. It isn't, most specifically the sanitariums. Elinor Burkett, a former AIDS reporter for the *Miami Herald* with extensive experience in Cuba and the author of *The Gravest Show on Earth: America in the Age of AIDS*, notes: "What's different in Cuba is that people don't think about individual rights. Most Americans think that when we're balancing social good with individual rights, we err toward the latter. Cubans are trained in the opposite mentality, so my friends in the sanitariums . . . believe there's a social good coming out of it." There is also the medical fact that isolation for HIV, a difficult-to-get virus, is unnecessary provided there are 1) testing and notification to alert those infected and 2) transmission education for them.

Nor is it to say that no exceptionalist methods work. On June 27, 1997, the American Medical Association emphatically supported needle exchange, a favorite exceptionalist method that clearly helps reduce HIV transmission. Nor is the exceptionalist weltanschauung completely wrong. In America, the abundant discrimination visited upon homosexuals and the HIV positive did indeed create problems for traditional public-health methods. However, the public-health answer is to challenge the discrimination, not eliminate good epidemiology.

Opposition to such epidemiology has, in this country, reached ludicrous proportions, actually compromising medical care. Miss Burkett offers her own personal example. "In the United States, when you go in for a surgical procedure, you get tested for everything, which is just good medicine—but not HIV. A few years ago, I had lymphoma. Here is a disease that is 63 times more common among HIV-positive people. I had just been tested and knew I was negative, but my doctors didn't know that. So I go in and I wait for them to suggest I get an HIV test. And I wait and I wait and I wait. And the day I'm starting chemotherapy I ask my doctor why he didn't test me. And he got very defensive. He said, 'Well, I can't test you without your permission, that's the law.' I asked: 'Well, why didn't you suggest it was medically wise?' I knew the answer perfectly well: I was a straight, white, upper-middle-class woman. But it was completely medically irresponsible, because as a doctor you are going to treat my lymphoma quite differently depending on whether I'm HIV positive or HIV negative. Because of these policies, we are giving *heart* transplants without routinely testing people. Which is insane. I just don't understand how you're going to practice good medicine without routine testing."

Shifting political alignments

From the point of view of HR-1062, what is interesting is that Miss Burkett is echoing the GP from Oklahoma almost word for word. He is a Christian Coalition Republican and she is a devout self-described "old lefty" with numerous gay friends who nevertheless will tell you, "These old [exceptionalist] policies were born out of a reality which, if it ever existed, certainly doesn't any more."

The Burkett/Coburn symmetry illustrates a subtle shifting of alignments. Dr. Thomas Coates, Professor of Medicine and Director of the Center for AIDS Prevention Studies at the University of California at San Francisco, is as adept at surviving in the cauldron of left-wing San Francisco AIDS politics as anyone. Dr. Coates recently supported traditionalist measures. His change of heart was prompted by the evidence from AIDS programs abroad: "In the end, the HIV and STD epidemics are unnecessary," he said. "No other industrialized country has these problems. Europe and Australia and New Zealand have gone after these diseases with traditionalist methods *and* with non-traditionalist, new methods supported by the exceptionalists, and have essentially taken care of them."

The AIDS organizations' resistance to traditionalism is still emphatic, but then cold hard reality is not their strong suit. These are the people who brought you the seductive lie that condoms are the universal answer to all diseases that ride on human sexuality. Gay men have swallowed this, but the condom solution has failed. Coburn contends—and while it is perhaps unprovable it is very interesting—that trust in condoms actually contributed to an *increase* in transmission of HIV and STDs through increased sexual activity multiplied by the condom breakage rate.

The condom solution has failed.

Moreover—and this should alarm the gay community—despite the current decline in the rate of HIV transmission among gay men, one must note that statistically we are still, as Michael Fumento put it, "the rats [carrying the] fleas of the new plague." Given human nature, today's decline and the desire to believe that the epidemic has been "conquered," accompanied by the inevitable slipping back into unsafe sex and renewed promiscuity, may mean our regaining plague leadership in the future. Gabriel Rotello, a *Newsday* columnist and a gay man who has bucked AIDS dogma, noted in his book *Sexual Ecology* that the backlash has already begun. "Editorial boards . . . have moved to distance themselves from gay-run AIDS groups they once unquestioningly supported. Liberal politicians have begun asking tough questions in private while becoming noncommittal in public. Friends of gay people have begun to wonder aloud at the high rates of unsafe sex and transmission."

A difficult problem

In the end, the public-health response to AIDS is not an easy problem. Do we, by implementing effective policies, hurt the small number of individuals who will, inevitably, be outed and risk being fired from jobs, and thereby save many times their number from exposure to a devastating virus? Or do we hurt a large number of individuals by refusing to implement policies to combat the disease that will poison their bodies? One of Dr. Coburn's allies answers the question succinctly: "The AIDS community forgets that the ultimate violation of civil rights is being infected with AIDS." And 35 times more deaths per capita under an exceptionalist regime indicates that, somewhere, something went very, very wrong.

Back on Capitol Hill, Tom Coburn will spend the fall of 1997 working hard on his bill. It aims to chart a new course on AIDS policy, but it is a very delicate matter when under the old course thousands of people have already died and thousands more are sick and the figures seem all out of proportion and you have this nagging little question of responsibility. Dr. Coburn might prefer not to get into it at all (it could certainly complicate the debate), but the fact is, and he knows it, that the mere existence of his bill is forcing an entire political community to step up and calmly respond to the accusation of mass manslaughter. They are not particularly calm at the moment. But you would be hysterical, too, if someone said to you, "Through everything you've worked for, by everything you believe, and with everything you've fought to maintain, you have helped to kill a hundred thousand human beings."

10

Civil Rights Must Be Protected in the Fight Against AIDS

American Civil Liberties Union

The American Civil Liberties Union is a national organization that works to defend civil rights and liberties guaranteed by law and the U.S. Constitution.

Some people have proposed that public health authorities should be given the names of all people who test positive for HIV, the virus that causes AIDS. Such a change to the present system of voluntary and anonymous AIDS testing would endanger privacy rights and would do little to end the AIDS epidemic. People fearing social prejudice will be reluctant to get tested for HIV/AIDS, preventing them from getting treated and hampering efforts to track the spread of the disease. An alternative approach would be to use a system of special codes called unique identifiers to track the epidemic while preserving the privacy of individuals. Such a formula would prevent any conflict between civil liberties and public health.

Recently, there have been renewed calls for HIV surveillance, and specifically for reporting the names of all those who test positive for HIV to public health authorities. Proponents of HIV surveillance and name reporting frequently suggest that there is a conflict between the privacy rights of individuals who have or may have HIV and the public health needs of the country, and that individual civil liberties must take a back seat in order to effectively battle the spread of HIV and AIDS.

In the public debate concerning society's response to the AIDS epidemic the American Civil Liberties Union has consistently advocated policies that protect the public health while respecting civil liberties and individual privacy. The ACLU recognizes that given the rapid speed with which HIV treatment, the social response to HIV and the disease itself change, every important social and legal policy about HIV must be under

Reprinted with permission from "HIV Surveillance and Name Reporting: A Public Health Case for Protecting Civil Liberties," a report by the American Civil Liberties Union, October 1997.

constant reexamination. There are no permanent answers. The ACLU also believes that policy must be based on cool examination of the best evidence we have, and not on ideology or visions of the world as we would like it to be. The ACLU is issuing this position paper now because the available evidence shows that, *when it comes to reporting the names of people with HIV, there is no conflict between public health and civil liberties.* Instead, the available evidence strongly suggests that public health measures that respect the privacy of individuals testing for HIV are more effective means of fighting the spread of HIV than intrusive measures like name reporting. Specifically, as discussed in more detail in this position paper, the evidence indicates that reporting the names of those who test positive for HIV will set back public health efforts. For this reason, the ACLU opposes name reporting.

Renewed calls for HIV surveillance are at least partly the result of new developments in the AIDS epidemic, primarily the emergence of promising new medical treatments. Proponents of name reporting argue that in the face of medical and other developments, it no longer makes sense to systematically track only AIDS cases, which represent the late stages of HIV disease; they argue that we must start to track HIV systematically from the point of infection.

The American Civil Liberties Union has consistently advocated policies that protect the public health while respecting civil liberties and individual privacy.

A number of propositions are generally advanced in support of HIV surveillance and name reporting*: (1) there is a need to monitor the spread of HIV and collect more accurate epidemiological data; (2) it would help better target prevention and public health efforts; (3) it would permit individuals with HIV to proactively link to appropriate health care services; (4) it would permit a more efficient allocation of AIDS funding; and (5) concerns about discrimination against people with HIV and AIDS are much reduced as a result of supposedly strong legal protections of confidentiality and against discrimination. Even though there are various methods for HIV surveillance that preserve the privacy of individuals with HIV, surveillance proponents generally argue that reporting the names of individuals who test positive for HIV is necessary for effective HIV surveillance.

The case for HIV surveillance may well be stronger at this juncture of the AIDS epidemic. However, while the reasons cited above may justify increased tracking of cases of HIV infection, they do not support name reporting for several reasons. First, while the goal of increased tracking of

---

*Proposals for HIV surveillance by name reporting can be divided generally into two groups. This paper uses the term "name reporting" to refer to both of them together. The first subgroup involves proposals in which reporting the names of all individuals who test positive for HIV would be required. This system, which would effectively eliminate anonymous HIV testing, is referred to in this paper as "mandatory name reporting." Some have suggested an HIV surveillance system in which name reporting is encouraged, but anonymous testing sites are maintained for those individuals who refuse to be tested by name. This system is referred to in this viewpoint as "hybrid reporting."

HIV infection is to bring those with HIV into the public health system and to obtain more accurate epidemiological data, name reporting will likely have the opposite effect. This is because the available evidence strongly suggests that eliminating anonymous HIV testing will discourage individuals from being tested, thus preventing their entrance into the public health system and hampering HIV tracking.

Second, name reporting is not essential to effectively monitor the epidemic, target prevention, link individuals with HIV to health care, and allocate AIDS funding. Existing HIV tracking mechanisms, including sentinel studies and incidence and prevalence surveys, help to accomplish these goals. And the use of unique identifiers (alphanumerical codes) provides an alternative means of reporting individual cases of HIV without using names.

Third, legal protections for people with HIV appear to be weaker than advocates of name reporting think they are. There are troubling examples of breaches of privacy in spite of the confidentiality protections that accompany name reporting in the states where it presently exists. And legal developments indicate that some courts do not believe that the Americans with Disabilities Act provides broad-based protection to people with HIV who are not seriously ill. It is, in short, not accurate to say that the fears of discrimination that appear to drive people away from testing are groundless.

Finally, given that we presently are unable or unwilling to provide access to anti-retroviral therapy and other forms of health care to individuals with HIV who are already seeking treatment, it is hard to see how imposition of names-based reporting is going to result in better health care for those individuals with HIV who are not yet in the health care system.

Therefore, the ACLU opposes name reporting as a means of tracking HIV unless and until: (1) it has been demonstrated that there is a strong need for additional HIV surveillance; (2) there is no alternative means to accomplish this surveillance; (3) we can honestly assure those who will be tested that protection from discrimination is real; and (4) serious efforts to deliver care to those who will be identified will be made. These conditions have not been satisfied.

Early history of HIV/AIDS

AIDS first emerged in the early 1980's as a health crisis among gay men, who began experiencing an onset of severe and unexplained health problems that quickly turned fatal. At the time there was no medical understanding of the emerging epidemic, and there was widespread societal fear about possible contagion. AIDS became a marker for gay men, and since many in the population held strong biases against gay people, a social stigma attached to AIDS that set the syndrome apart from other contagious diseases. Gay men with AIDS were fired from their jobs, lost their health insurance and their homes, were turned away by health care providers, and were ostracized by their families, either because of their mysterious health condition, their sexual orientation, or both.

Surveillance of AIDS cases, including reporting the names of persons diagnosed with AIDS to public health authorities, began almost immediately and with little fanfare. There were several reasons for this. First, name reporting was a public health response which had been used with some other sexually transmitted diseases. Second, individuals who were diagnosed with AIDS were already in the late stages of what we now know to be HIV disease, and were for the most part already participating in the health care system. Thus in a real sense they had already been "identified" as persons with AIDS. And finally, although an AIDS diagnosis and public dissemination of that information often triggered a hostile societal response, the harsh reality was that persons diagnosed with AIDS usually died quickly, and the struggle for survival overwhelmed any attempt at leading a "normal life."

HIV was not discovered until 1983, and testing for HIV antibodies became available only in the mid 1980's. At that time, surveillance of cases of HIV infection, as opposed to AIDS diagnosis, was opposed by advocacy groups and public health authorities. There was widespread recognition that gay men, people of color and IV drug users, the sub-populations found to be at highest risk for HIV infection as the epidemic developed, would flee from the public health system if they believed that their names were being reported to government agencies. In the absence of any effective cure or medical treatment for HIV infection, the arguments in favor of HIV surveillance were weak.

Recent developments

In the mid 1990s a number of factors have shifted the focus of epidemiological surveillance to the "front end" of the AIDS epidemic, HIV infection. New medical treatments in the form of combination therapy offer greater hope for healthier and longer lives for people with HIV. Research suggests that combination therapy is most effective if begun soon after infection, making it important that therapy be offered to people before they become severely ill. Moreover some research suggests that combination therapy, by drastically reducing the amount of virus an individual carries, lessens infectiousness.[1]

For the first time in a decade the number of deaths attributable to AIDS is decreasing. AIDS deaths declined 19 percent in the first nine months of 1996 compared to the same period in 1995.[2] Public health officials, while encouraged by this development, worry that individuals continue to become infected. As medical treatments prolong the lives of people with HIV and significantly delay the amount of time from infection to AIDS diagnosis, surveillance of AIDS cases tells us less and less about how HIV infection is developing and spreading.

In addition, as the AIDS epidemic nears the completion of its second decade, the early societal panic about AIDS has diminished. Legal protections for people with AIDS have improved, thanks largely to the passage of the Americans with Disabilities Act (ADA). Many cities have passed legislation specifically designed to prevent discrimination on the basis of HIV. Prominent celebrities have announced that they are HIV positive, and courageous AIDS activists have won broad admiration in many quarters of society. These developments have somewhat lessened fears that the inevitable result of infection with HIV was complete social isolation.

Against this background, calls for enhanced HIV surveillance, name reporting, and an end to so-called "AIDS exceptionalism" have begun to emerge.[3] Even though there are numerous means of conducting HIV surveillance while maintaining the anonymity of persons with HIV, including the use of unique identifiers, sentinel studies, and incidence and prevalence studies, some have championed name reporting as a "traditional" response to infectious diseases which should be used with AIDS.

Twenty-seven states have already implemented name reporting HIV surveillance.[4] But these states represent only 24 percent of the AIDS cases that have been reported to the CDC.[5] "High incidence" states have thus far [as of October 1997] refused to adopt name reporting in the face of strong opposition from community groups and public health officials.

Proposals for name reporting take numerous forms. The unifying element is reporting the names of individuals who test positive for HIV to a government agency. Most often proposals for name reporting require individuals being tested for HIV (or an equivalent test, such as viral load or CD4) to provide their name, contact, and demographic information when they seek an HIV test. If the individual tests positive for HIV antibodies, then her/his name is reported to public health officials. Name reporting schemes generally have provisions designed to protect the confidentiality of the individual with HIV.

Name reporting is bad public policy

A. Name Reporting Is Bad Policy if It Discourages People from Being Tested for HIV, and the Available Evidence Shows That It Does

The available evidence strongly suggests that name reporting is a counterproductive public health measure that will cause individuals to avoid HIV testing. Numerous studies indicate that individuals avoid HIV testing that is not anonymous because they do not have faith that test results will remain confidential and because they fear the stigma and discrimination that is often associated with HIV and AIDS. One study found that over 60% of individuals tested anonymously would not have tested if their names were reported to public health officials.[6] By contrast, anonymous testing encourages individuals to seek testing in the belief that they will be able to control the dissemination of information about their HIV status. People are more likely to be voluntarily tested for HIV if the testing is anonymous.[7]

Anonymous testing also reduces the period of time that individuals delay testing. Research indicates that the availability of anonymous testing reduces the average delay between deciding to get tested and actually going for the test by more than one half, from a mean of 12 months to a mean of 5 months.[8] Testing associated with name reporting (confidential testing) deters people from discovering their HIV status.

Of course, HIV testing is of little use if the person tested does not return for his or her results. The available data indicates that individuals who test at locations with name reporting are much less likely to return for their results than individuals who are anonymously tested. An analysis of HIV testing in North Carolina found that 30.3% of testees undergoing confidential testing did not return, while only 8.2% of anonymous testers did not retrieve their results.[9] In Colorado, a testing survey showed that 95% of anonymous testers retrieved their results, but only 85% of confidential testees returned.[10]

The deterrent effect of name reporting is most pronounced in the very populations with the greatest need for preventive intervention: gay and bisexual men, people of color, intravenous drug users, and sex workers. Research indicates that gay men are more likely to be aware of name reporting requirements and, as a result, to avoid testing altogether.[11] One study found that half of the men who were tested anonymously would not have been tested at all if only confidential testing were offered.[12] In South Carolina, after anonymous testing was eliminated the number of men who have sex with men who were tested for HIV dropped by 51%.[13] The converse is also true: once anonymous testing is offered, more gay and bisexual men will be tested. Oregon, for example, reported a 125% increase in the demand for HIV testing once the option of anonymous testing was provided.[14] Fear of discrimination and stigmatization is so strong among gay and bisexual men, they will travel to other states if necessary to preserve their anonymity. One South Carolina AIDS service agency reported that 40% of the people it serves were tested out of state.[15] If gay and bisexual men do test confidentially, as opposed to anonymously, they often will wait longer to do so.[16] Given the high seroprevalence rate among gay and bisexual men, delays are counterproductive to the public health goal of HIV prevention.[17]

Name reporting is also likely to deter HIV testing by African-Americans and Latinos.[18] The rate of HIV infection is increasing rapidly among people of color.[19] Given this country's history of race discrimination in the guise of public health initiatives, minority communities often distrust coercive public health programs. Mandatory names reporting would only exacerbate this distrust. Researchers from the New York City Department of Health found that 22% of African-American and Hispanic participants would not be tested for HIV if their names were reported to public health officials.[20] One clinician commented that mandatory name reporting "will be the final blow" alienating minority women from clinicians and the health care system, causing them to go "underground fast."[21]

Other groups are also deterred from HIV testing by name reporting. Intravenous drug users and sex workers, many of whose primary contact with government has been through the criminal justice system, are more likely to test anonymously. One study found a 56% increase in HIV testing among female sex workers and a 17% increase among intravenous drug users when anonymous testing was an option.[22] Women, in general, are often wary of mandatory names reporting schemes. One study found that mandatory names reporting led to a 31% decline in the number of women agreeing to an HIV test as they sought Ob/Gyn care.[23]

When it comes to reporting the names of people with HIV, there is no conflict between public health and civil liberties.

Some proponents of HIV surveillance have proposed maintaining anonymous testing, but imposing the mandatory name reporting requirement on medical providers, as a means of avoiding testing deterrence. This is not an acceptable solution, since it simply shifts the deterrence problem away from testing and instead deters people from entering treatment. In a recent survey of individuals testing for HIV in Los Angeles County, 22.6% of survey participants said they would delay treatment until they were actually sick if their doctor were required to report their name to public health authorities.[24]

The available evidence strongly suggests that name reporting is a counterproductive health measure that will cause individuals to avoid HIV testing.

It has been suggested by some that name reporting should be adopted but that anonymous testing should be preserved for those who do not want to be reported. It is far from clear that this type of hybrid reporting would accomplish any of the goals advanced for increased surveillance. Moreover, to make that system work and not deter people from testing, people must understand their options. Individuals would have to be advised that they have the option of anonymous testing, and anonymous testing sites would have to provide the same array of services provided by sites that record the name of the testee for reporting purposes (confidential testing sites). Medical providers could not be required to report the names of patients who are HIV positive against the patients' will, since that would deter treatment as opposed to testing. The history of minority communities and public health suggests that a system like this would not truly reassure those who need to be tested. If proponents of name reporting believe this option, faithfully implemented, would advance the goals of increased surveillance, it ought to be tried on a trial basis and the effect on both reporting and deterrence assessed before it is widely used.

In sum, the available evidence indicates that rather than helping to control the spread of HIV and AIDS and encouraging earlier medical intervention, name reporting is likely to lead to decreased testing by those who most need it. That means that far from advancing the goal proponents offer for increased surveillance—more accurate information and earlier medical intervention—name reporting is likely to defeat them.

B. Testee Fear of HIV Name Reporting Cannot Be Dismissed as Irrational

Many individuals apparently fear taking an HIV test that is not anonymous, as the evidence discussed in the last section shows. It is worth stressing that the perception of the testee is what matters most. If that perception is going to prevent an individual from testing, it does not matter whether the perception is based on misinformation, reality, or some combination of the two. The sad truth, however, is that these fears cannot be dismissed as irrational.

At the heart of the fear is concern about discrimination on the basis of HIV status, and this concern is real. Laws cannot prevent family and friends from abandoning a loved one because she has HIV or because he is gay. And legal developments indicate that persons with HIV still have reason to worry about even those types of discrimination that the law is designed to address. Although it had once been assumed that the Americans with Disabilities Act (ADA) provided broad legal protections from discrimination against anyone with HIV, according to some federal courts this is not the case. A federal appeals court has ruled that the ADA does not protect people with HIV who have not yet developed serious health problems, even if they have suffered from discrimination.[25] Another federal appeals court has held that the ADA does not protect many people with either HIV or AIDS from discrimination in insurance.[26] Thus, the anti-discrimination protections supposedly provided by the ADA may be becoming illusory for people with HIV. [Editor's note: The U.S. Supreme Court ruled in June 1998 in the case of *Bragdon v. Abbot* that the ADA protects from discrimination people who have HIV but show no symptoms of AIDS.]

It is unlikely that the fears of individuals at high risk for HIV can be overcome by promises that name reporting will be accompanied by privacy protections. Minority communities are often distrustful of public health authorities and coercive public health programs.[27] Existing privacy protections have not prevented breaches of confidentiality from occurring. In one example, thieves stole a computer containing the names of 60 persons with AIDS from a public health office in Sacramento, California.[28] As this incident demonstrated, computerization and modern security devices do not provide complete security. Moreover, the complexity of modern computer systems and data banks will inevitably lead to mistakes that are at once common and difficult to correct.[29] These general problems take on special significance in the context of HIV surveillance, given the sensitivity of HIV-related information.

In Florida, a computer disk containing the names of 4000 people with AIDS was discovered in the parking lot of a bar.

Despite the frequent claim that this has never happened, confidentiality is breached. Agencies cannot control how authorized personnel use the data to which they have access, creating a risk of both inadvertent and intentional confidentiality breaches.[30] Personnel with access to names include federal, state and local public health administrators, HIV-related social service and medical professionals, field service staff, and, due to efforts to integrate tuberculosis and HIV surveillance, non-HIV public health officials. Carelessness and simple human error can have serious consequences. In Florida, a computer disk containing the names of 4000 people with AIDS was discovered in the parking lot of a bar. Apparently it belonged to an AIDS surveillance case worker who misplaced it.[31] In New York, a log containing the names of 500 people who were tested for HIV "vanished" from a clinic.[32] Almost a week later, authorities still did not know if the log was stolen, thrown out, misplaced or destroyed. The Federal Bureau of Investigation has admittedly used improperly obtained HIV information, and local law enforcement agencies have disclosed HIV status to neighbors, prison inmates, and broadcast the names of people with HIV over police radios.[33]

Moreover, present assurances of confidentiality cannot prevent later evisceration of privacy guarantees. Once public health officials have compiled a list of individuals who are HIV-positive, there is no way to safeguard the list from overzealous public health efforts and misguided political mischief in the future. Just as a legislature may enact confidentiality provisions, so too may it later create exceptions or revoke protections in toto. This almost occurred in 1991 when the state of Illinois passed a law that directed the Department of Health to identify all HIV-positive health care workers by comparing the state's confidential lists of persons with HIV against the records of health care licenses. Any patient of a health care worker who engaged in invasive medical procedures (surgery) while HIV-positive was to be contacted. This government-sponsored violation of privacy was approved despite widespread recognition that the policy would do little to advance the public health. Although never funded due to intense opposition, this experience demonstrates the inherently precarious nature of a seemingly ironclad confidentiality guarantee.

Finally, it is too early to know if the emergence of promising new medical treatments (should the promise hold) will increase the impetus to be tested, and the extent to which they will ameliorate or eliminate the well-documented deterrent effect that occurs when anonymous testing is eliminated. It is, therefore, simply not responsible to glibly assume that the existence of these therapies removes the public health problems created by the elimination of anonymous testing. Moreover, it is reasonable to assume that, in any event, combination therapy will increase the attractiveness of testing only for those individuals who believe they can get access to the treatment if they test positive for HIV. Combination therapy is not made available to all those who presently need it, as has been painfully demonstrated by the experiences of AIDS Drug Assistance Program (ADAP) programs in Mississippi and other states that have been forced to cut people with HIV off medication due to a lack of funds. Low income people who do not have the means to pay for medication could reasonably conclude that, even if they test positive for HIV, they will not be able to access appropriate medical care.[34]

In sum, the fears that drive people away from HIV testing with name reporting are not groundless. To eliminate them, we need more than education; we need solid anti-discrimination protection and real availability of treatment for the poor and the uninsured. Name reporting is not appropriate until we make real progress toward those two goals.

Unique identifiers a better alternative

The desire for more comprehensive HIV surveillance can be accommodated without name reporting. HIV surveillance is already being conducted through sentinel studies and prevalence and incidence studies, and those efforts can be expanded. In addition, systematic HIV surveillance can be implemented through the use of a system of unique identifiers.

Unique identifiers are numeric and alphanumeric codes that are used to identify a particular individual. We use these every day in the form of social security numbers, driver's license numbers, and account numbers, among others. In the context of HIV testing, the concept is to create a code that identifies only one person and to associate the HIV test result with that unique identifier, rather than with the name of the individual. The code may be reported to public health authorities, providing accurate epidemiological data regarding HIV infection rates along with various demographic indicators. But because the code cannot be traced back to the person tested, the anonymity of the testee is preserved.

With computerized encryption and modern technology, unique identifiers may offer a viable alternative to name reporting. There are sound reasons to pursue this option if expanded HIV surveillance is desired. First, by preserving the anonymity of the testee, a unique identifier system encourages individuals to be tested and enlists the support of community organizations that are opposed to name reporting. Second, it is at least possible that unique identifier systems may ultimately provide better epidemiological data than name reporting confidential testing.[35] In a unique identifier system, an individual will most likely use the same code for each test (e.g. birth date and the last four digits of social security number). With one unique identifier composed of intimate information (so the individual remembers it), a repeat tester can be identified as such and not double counted. The accuracy of names-based reporting, by contrast, depends upon whether the testee uses his or her real name, and the available evidence suggests that many people who are required to give their name when taking an HIV test use a pseudonym to hide their identity.[36] While distrust causes testees to use pseudonyms in confidential testing, in anonymous testing there is no incentive to create more than one unique identifier.

> *We need solid anti-discrimination protection and real availability of treatment for the poor and uninsured.*

Two states, Maryland and Texas, presently use unique identifier systems to track HIV cases. The experiences of both states should be analyzed to determine the benefits and drawbacks of unique identifiers, and to identify what work must be done to make them effective tools for HIV surveillance.

It appears that developing effective unique identifier systems will require the investment of significant time and resources. But given the evidence that name reporting will discourage testing, particularly among those who most need it for themselves and for accurate surveillance, it remains the most sensible option today.

Legitimate fears of discrimination

There may come a time when HIV is so unremarkable a part of our social landscape, and care for it so routinely available to those who need it, that no one will reasonably fear being identified as a person with HIV. But we are nowhere close to that time yet. On the contrary, the best evidence we have suggests that those who most need HIV testing are afraid of name reporting because they fear discrimination. Moreover, we know those fears are not groundless.

We cannot honestly allay these fears unless we truly provide people with HIV the protection from discrimination we have been promising them. We cannot honestly use the availability of new treatment to get people to overcome their fears of discrimination unless we are ready to make treatment available. Since we have done neither, we cannot honestly tell people they should overcome their fears of testing. Under these circumstances, name reporting is not appropriate.

Notes

1. R. Royce et al., *Sexual Transmission of HIV: Current Concepts*, 336 New Eng. J. of Med. 1072 (1997).

2. L.K. Altman, *AIDS deaths drop 19% in U.S., continuing a heartening trend*, New York Times, July 15, 1997, at A1.

3. The term "AIDS exceptionalism" has been coined by some advocates of HIV surveillance and name reporting to refer to the fact that traditional intrusive public health measures, such as mandatory name reporting, have not been systematically applied to HIV infection. The term is an unfortunate misnomer, since the public health response to all infectious diseases has not been uniform and since there is no indication that a "one-size-fits-all" approach to all public health problems is effective.

4. See Appendix II [available at www.aclu.org/issues/aids/namereport.html].

5. Centers for Disease Control and Prevention, HIV/AIDS Surveillance Report, 1997, Vol. 9, No. 1.

6. Susan M. Kegeles et al., Many People Who Seek Anonymous HIV-Antibody Testing Would Avoid it Under Other Circumstances, 4 AIDS 585, 586 (1990).

7. Kathleen Irwin et al., *The Acceptability of Voluntary HIV Antibody Testing In the United States: A Decade of Lessons Learned*, AIDS, vol. 10, no. 14, 1707, 1711 (1996); Geoffrey Reed et al., *The Impact of Mandatory Name Reporting on HIV Testing and Treatment*, Poster Presentation for the XI International Conference on AIDS (July 1996); Douglas Hirano et al., *Anonymous HIV Testing: The Impact of Availability on Demand in Arizona*, 84 AM. J. PUB. HEALTH 2008, 2010 (1994).

8. Laura Fehrs et al., *Trial of Anonymous Versus Confidential Human Immunodeficiency Virus Testing*, 2 LANCET 391 (1988).

9. Irva Hertz Picciotto et al., *HIV Test-Seeking Before and After the Restriction of Anonymous Testing in North Carolina*, 86 AM. J. PUB. HEALTH 1446, 1448 (1996).

10. Richard E. Hoffman et al., Colorado Department of Health Division of Disease Control and Environmental Epidemiology, HIV Anonymous Test Site Evaluations 7 (1992).

11. HIRANO, *supra* note 5, at 2009; KEGELES, *supra* note 4.

12. Susan M. Kegeles et al., *Mandatory Reporting of HIV Testing Would Deter Men from Being Tested*, 261 JAMA 1275 (1989).

13. W.D. Johnson et al., The Impact of Mandatory Reporting on HIV Seropositive Persons in South Carolina (1988) (Presented at the Fourth International Conference on AIDS, Stockholm, Sweden).

14. FEHRS et al., *supra* note 6.

15. JOHNSON, *supra* note 14.

16. HIRANO, *supra* note 5, at 2009.

17. *Id.* at 2010.

18. While people of color are discussed separately from gay and bisexual men in this position paper because of the high rates of HIV infection in many communities of color, it is worth noting that the two groups are not mutually exclusive—i.e. many gay and bisexual men of color are infected with HIV.

19. See, e.g., Allan P. Frank et al., *Anonymous HIV Testing Using Home Collection and Telemedicine Counseling: A Multicenter Evaluation*, 157 ARCHIVES INTERNAL MED. 309 (1997).

20. E. Fordyce et al., *Mandatory Reporting of Human Immunodeficiency Virus Testing Would Deter Blacks and Hispanics from Being Tested*, 262 JAMA 349 (1989).

21. Letter from B. Joyce Simpson, RN, MPH, to Robert M. Greenstein, Director of Division of Human Genetics, University of Connecticut Health Center (November 30, 1992) (on file with the ACLU AIDS/HIV Project).

22. FEHRS et al., *supra* note 6.

23. B. Lo et al., AIDS Screening: Who is Willing to be Tested (1988) (Presented at the Fourth International Conference on AIDS, Stockholm, Sweden).

24. Geoffrey Reed et al., *The Impact of Mandatory Name Reporting on HIV Testing and Treatment*, Poster Presentation for the XI International Conference on AIDS (July 1996).

25. *Runnebaum v. Nationsbank of Maryland*, __F.3d__, 1997 WL 465301 (4th Cir. Aug. 15, 1997) (*en banc*).

26. *Parker v. Metropolitan Life Insurance Company*, __F.3d__, (6th Cir. Aug. 1, 1997) (*en banc*).

27. See e.g., Woodrow Jones, An Overview Of Health Care Issues In Black America, in *Black Health Care*, Jones & Rice, eds., 1987.

28. Richard C. Paddock, *Thieves Steal Computer Containing Confidential List of 60 AIDS Victims*, L.A. Times, July 9, 1987, at 3.

29. Bob Davis, *Abusive Computers: As Government Keeps More Tabs on People False Accusations Rise*, Wall St. J., August 20, 1987, at 1.

30. Robert Trigaux, *Leak sparks security fears*, St. Petersburg Times, September 20, 1996, at 1A. *See also* Lawrence O. Gostin, *Health Information Privacy*, 80 Cornell L. Rev 451, 493 (1995) ("It is the proliferation of . . . legitimate users of information that pose the greatest risk to informational privacy").

31. Sue Landry, *AIDS list is out*, St. Petersburg Times, September 20, 1996, at 1A.

32. *Log, Said to List AIDS Test-Takers, Is Lost*, N.Y. Times, April 23, 1987, at A21.

33. *Doe v. Attorney General of the United States*, 941 F. 2d 780 (9th Cir. 1991); *Doe v. Borough of Barrington*, 729 F. Supp. 376 (D.N.J. 1990); *Woods v. White*, 689 F. Supp. 874 (W.D.Wis. 1988); details on Union City, California's practice of broadcasting the names of people with HIV on radios

used by police, fire, and emergency medical workers are on file with the ACLU AIDS Project.

34. Sheryl Gay Stolberg, *AIDS Drugs Elude the Grasp of Many of the Poor*, New York Times, October 14, 1997, at A22.

35. Anna Forbes, *Mandatory Name-based HIV Reporting: Impact and Alternatives*, AIDS Policy & Law, May 1996.

36. T. Hoxworth et al., *Anonymous HIV Testing: Does It Attract Clients Who Would Not Seek Confidential Testing?* 9 AIDS PUB. POL'Y J. 182 (1994).

11

Gay Sexual Promiscuity Contributed to the AIDS Epidemic

Gabriel Rotello

Journalist and gay activist Gabriel Rotello is a former columnist for New York Newsday *and author of* Sexual Ecology: AIDS and the Destiny of Gay Men.

AIDS became an epidemic for American gay men in the 1980s because of the collective sexual behavior of that group, which included practices such as multiple concurrent partners, versatile anal sex, and widespread promiscuity centered in commercial sex establishments. The gay community must rethink its position on what gay liberation means in terms of sexual behavior.

Experts argue that the spread of the human immunodeficiency virus (HIV) among sexually active gay men in the early eighties resulted from a fatal confluence of the biology of HIV and the collective behavior of gay men. While the invention of safer sex in the form of the condom code is based on the simple idea that HIV is transmitted by infected body fluids, the reality is considerably more complex. HIV is indeed spread through body fluids, but virtually all sexually active people transmit body fluids, and very few produce rates of HIV transmission remotely approaching those of gay men. To understand why gay sexual ecology interacted with HIV in such a disastrous way, we need to look at the range of factors that influenced HIV transmission in the gay world.

Multipartner anal sex

Many people, including many gay men, presume that anal sex itself was the overriding factor that led to the extraordinary levels of infection in the gay population. However, it appears that the difference in risk between anal and vaginal sex is nowhere near sufficient to account for the several-thousandfold difference in HIV prevalence between gay men and comparable heterosexuals in the developed world. True, the rectum is somewhat more susceptible to infection than the vagina or the mouth, but not by very much. So the reason that anal sex led to catastrophic levels of infection in the gay population seems to have less to do with anal sex per se, and more to do with specific ways that gay men practiced it.

The primary factor that led to increased HIV transmission was anal sex combined with multiple partners, particularly in concentrated core groups. By the seventies there is little doubt that for those in the most sexually active core groups, multipartner anal sex had become the main event. Michael Callen, both an avid practitioner and a careful observer of life in the gay fast lane, believed that this was a "historically unprecedented aspect" of the gay sexual revolution. "In the urban gay fast lane of the '70s, the expectation was that fucking would take place," he wrote. "If you didn't fuck, you were thought odd." Callen, by the way, did not believe that this was essential to homosexuality or homosexuals. "Fucking is, for most gay men, an acquired taste," he wrote, which nonetheless "became more the rule than the exception, at least in the fast lane."[1]

> *The primary factor that led to increased HIV transmission was anal sex combined with multiple partners.*

A number of theories have been put forward in attempts to explain how something often considered a highly intimate activity came to be practiced with very large numbers of partners in certain core groups. One is that gay men were finally turning to each other for sex, especially in safe spaces like baths where the number of potential partners was maximal and the danger of interruption was minimal. This combination of higher self-esteem and greater safety created a powerful impetus toward greater intimacy. Another was that improved hygiene and available cures for venereal diseases made men feel safer about fucking. Still another was that the "loosen up" ethic of the sixties and seventies prompted a general move toward less self-restraint and greater sexual experimentation among both gays and straights. In addition, some have argued that as gay men came to consider their sexuality as equivalent to heterosexuality, they came to believe that anal sex ought to be as central to their sexual lives as vaginal sex is to straights. Still others have pointed out that many gay men first developed their sexual expectations from porn films, where the most common plot is that partners meet, they have oral sex, and then they have anal sex. Some argue that this influenced many gay men to believe that anal sex was simply expected, even in anonymous encounters and one-night stands.

Probably all of these factors played a role, but whatever the case, many researchers consider the combination of anal sex with multiple partners in tightly concentrated circles of individuals to have been the single most vital element in amplifying AIDS. Some epidemiologists now speculate that if the most sexually active core of gay men had confined themselves to oral sex or mutual masturbation with large numbers of partners, and had reserved anal sex for longer-term relationships, things would have turned out very differently.

Insertive/receptive "versatility"

In the middle of the century, and particularly in the sixties and seventies, gay men began doing something that appears rare in sexual history: They began to abandon strict role separation in sex and alternately play both the insertive and receptive roles, a practice sometimes called versatility.

In most cultures, male-to-male sexual relations were stratified and people played very defined roles. Sometimes, as David Greenberg writes in *The Construction of Homosexuality*, the stratification was based primarily on age, as when "the older partner takes a role defined as active or masculine; the younger, a role defined as passive or female."[2] In other societies roles are not based on age as much as on outward appearances of gender—as in the macho/queen dichotomy of many Latin American societies today. In such societies anal sex is highly structured, with the "homosexual" partner always playing the feminine, bottom role and the "macho" partner being the masculine top. The same separation also applied to early-twentieth-century New York, where the "fairy" or "queer" partner virtually always fellated the (presumably) straight partner.

As modern gay sexual culture emerged in the middle of the twentieth century, however, gay men began to consider this role separation a form of self-oppression. As more and more gay men began having sex with each other rather than with trade, and as more and more adopted anal sex as part of their sexual repertoire, activists called upon men to strive for sexual equality and reject strict role separation. Carl Wittman's "A Gay Manifesto," perhaps the most influential gay lib essay from the early seventies, was explicit on this point. In the section headed "On Positions and Roles" Wittman wrote:

> Much of our sexuality has been perverted through mimicry of straights, and warped from self-hatred. These sexual perversions are basically anti-gay:
>
> *"I like to make it with straight guys."*
> *"I'm not gay but I like to be 'done.'"*
> *"I like to fuck, but I don't want to be fucked."*
> *"I don't like to be touched above the neck. "*
>
> This is role playing at its worst; we must transcend these roles. We strive for democratic, mutual, reciprocal sex.[3]

For Wittman and many others, the stratification of sex roles was a relic of an oppressive past. As the seventies progressed, this rejection of role-playing became so pronounced that in a sense versatility itself became a kind of role: Those who disliked versatility for whatever reason began to feel embarrassed to admit it, since such reticence was now perceived by some as almost an affront to homosexuality. Whether one considers this a socially liberating development or just another form of sexual conformity, it seems to have had enormous consequences for gay sexual ecology.

To achieve maximum efficiency in transmission, sexually transmitted diseases (STDs) need to circulate freely within a sexual ecosystem. But because HIV is difficult to transmit and generally needs to be injected directly into the body and bloodstream, it is much easier for the insertive partner to infect the receptive one than the other way around. This creates what some epidemiologists call the "dead-end factor" that inhibits transmission from women to men in the developed world. In the absence of mitigating factors the virus is likely to hit a dead end wherever strict role separation is practiced. As we have seen, the dead-end factor is mitigated in parts of the Third World where men frequently have venereal sores that allow the virus to enter their bloodstreams directly. It also seems mitigated among uncircumcised men, since the tissue of the foreskin seems particularly susceptible to HIV infection and since the foreskin creates a reservoir where HIV can linger for long enough to enter the body.

Nowhere was the dead-end factor canceled out more efficiently, however, than where the gay practice of insertive/receptive "versatility" was widely adopted. Now the same person into whom HIV was injected could himself switch roles and become the injector into others, who themselves could receive the microbe passively and then reverse positions and pass it along. Mathematical models of the epidemic have stressed the central importance of this factor in the dissemination of HIV among gay men.[4]

Concurrency

Having multiple partners heightens the risk of transmission for any sexually transmitted disease, but not all forms of multiple partnering are equally risky. We have already seen how multipartnerism in core groups can amplify risk. Researchers calculate that there is also an enormous difference in risk between those who have multiple partners in a serial or a concurrent fashion.

Serial multipartnerism, which can also be called serial monogamy, means having partners one at a time. You become involved with someone, remain monogamous with that person while you're together, then break up and find a new partner with whom you are again monogamous for the duration of the relationship. *Concurrent multipartnerism* means having partners more or less interchangeably. Mathematical models have demonstrated that these two different styles create enormously different opportunities for disease transmission. Even if people in one population have an average of, say, twelve partners per year concurrently, and those in another population have the same number of partners but have them in a serial fashion, the concurrent population can suffer a rate of total disease transmission from 10 to 100 times higher than the serial population.[5]

To illustrate how this might work with a virus like HIV, let's compare two hypothetical men who both have twelve partners per year. The man who mixes his partners concurrently—let's call him Joe—goes back and forth among his twelve partners throughout the year, while Tom has his twelve partners in a linear fashion, taking one exclusive lover each month, then breaking up with that person, taking up with a new lover for a month, and so on.

Let's say that of Joe's twelve concurrent partners, Partner Ten is infected with HIV. Partner Ten is not very infectious, so although Joe has sex with all of his partners randomly from January through December, he does not become infected by Partner Ten until October. Once Joe is infected, however, he becomes highly infectious himself, as people newly

infected with HIV tend to be. Since he is still having concurrent sexual relations with all eleven of his other partners, he can now quickly and easily transmit his new infection to any of the other partners in his circle. As
a result, throughout the rest of October, November, and December, several or perhaps even most of his other partners become infected.

---

*To achieve maximum efficiency in transmission, STDs
need to circulate freely within a sexual ecosystem.*

Tom also has twelve partners that year, but has them one at a time.
Tom's Partner Ten is also HIV-positive and mildly infectious, and Tom
also becomes infected by this partner in October, at which point Tom becomes highly infectious. But while Tom can easily pass his new infection
along to his next two lovers, Partners Eleven and Twelve, he cannot pass
it along to Partners One through Nine, since he is no longer having sex
with them. So even though Joe and Tom both have twelve partners that
year, and even though the circumstances of their infection are the same—
infection by Partner Ten in the tenth month of the year—their abilities to
transmit their infection are vastly different. While that difference seems
notable in individuals, imagine how it would be further magnified if all
of Joe's partners are also concurrent with twelve other partners, all of
whom are also concurrent with twelve other partners, and so on, while
all of Tom's partners practice serial monogamy.

Among core groups of gay men, concurrency was the overwhelming
rule. Indeed, the urban gay culture of the seventies and early eighties so
avidly promoted and celebrated concurrency—in the baths and sex clubs,
among circles of "fuck buddies," and so on—that even many men in
long-term committed relationships saw little reason why they should not
engage in concurrent relations with others. Men frequenting bars, bathhouses, and sex clubs and having anonymous sex with dozens or even
hundreds of partners were mixing them together in what, from a virus's
point of view, would be the most efficient possible way. It is impossible
from today's vantage to go back and determine precisely the extent to
which sexual concurrency increased transmission among gay men, but
some investigators now believe that the prevalence of concurrency amplified transmission among gay men by factors of 10 to 100 times.

Viral load

One of the reasons that concurrent partners are so much more likely to
transmit HIV than serial partners has to do with a factor of HIV infection
known as viremia, or viral load. Viral load varies widely in the sexual fluids of HIV-positive men. For example, some studies indicate that there is
detectable HIV in the semen of less than 30 percent of all HIV-infected
men.[6] Of this group an even smaller percentage appears to have a viral
load hundreds of times higher than the average infectious HIV-positive
man. This very high level of viremia typically occurs at two times during
the course of HIV disease: at the very beginning, in the months after infection, and again near the end, when the virus has overwhelmed the

body's immune system. During the initial period, which can last up to six months, the invading HIV blooms throughout the body of its new host almost unchecked, and the newly infected person can have a viremia level many hundreds of times greater than will be typical later on. In all likelihood, this is the period when people are most able to transmit HIV.

Within several months of initial infection, however, the immune system mounts a more effective response. The body begins manufacturing millions of T cells to counterattack the virus, and eventually this counterattack dramatically lowers the level of free-floating HIV in the blood and other bodily fluids. The surviving HIV retreats into certain areas of the body, such as the lymph system, where it engages in a long battle of attrition with the immune system. During this period, which typically lasts for several years, the level of free-floating virus remains comparatively low, and the infected person is thought to be much less likely to transmit infection during sex. This is not to say that such a person *cannot* transmit infection. Indeed, transmissions during this period have been well documented. But the odds seem somewhat lower than they were during primary infection.

Eventually, however, HIV is able to mount a final assault of its own, manufacturing billions of virions a day to replace those lost in the battle with the immune system. At this point things begin to tip in favor of the virus. The level of viral replication overwhelms the ability to combat it, HIV swarms throughout the body, the level of viremia in bodily fluids rises to levels comparable to those in the first several months of infection, and the infected individual usually begins to suffer from opportunistic infections. At this stage the person again develops a heightened ability to transmit HIV, and this time that ability appears to be for keeps.

This limited period in which a person is highly infectious could have a significant impact on transmission in populations that have concurrent partners. What it implies is that for HIV to have the greatest chance of spreading, an infected person not only needs to have unsafe sex with lots of partners, but to do so within the relatively brief time that he is highly infectious. In other words, lots of concurrent partners in the briefest possible time span will equal the greatest chance of epidemic spread. Precisely those conditions were most prevalent among the core of gay men who had large numbers of partners. If, however, a person remains monogamous during the peak period of infectiousness, and especially if that person remains monogamous with the very person who infected him or her, that highly infectious period is wasted from the virus's point of view. Such would tend to be the case where people practice serial monogamy.

Other STDs

Researchers have recognized that a number of other factors make gay men more susceptible to viral infection, both by lowering the body's natural immunity and by placing people in the position where they are more likely to encounter infection. High on the list of other factors facilitating HIV's spread in the gay population was the enormous increase in other STDs. Increased STD infection raises the risk of HIV transmission by causing venereal sores that allow direct viral access to the bloodstream, and by placing a ready pool of easily infected white blood cells at the point of entry. Most middle-class gay men who contracted lots of STDs had ready access to health care and usually did not walk around for long with untreated venereal sores. Ironically, however, their immune systems were depleted by repeated courses of antibiotics prescribed to fight other STD infections. Such continuous use of powerful antibiotics can compromise the immune system in ways that make infection by many different microbes, including HIV, far more likely. So, in this way, the very access to quality health care that helped make the gay sexual revolution possible contributed to the rapid spread of HIV.

Substance abuse

Drinking and drug abuse also lower immunity and tend to increase risky behaviors. Alcohol had long been an important part of gay social life, partly because of the central role that bars played in fostering a gay identity, partly because those engaging in deeply stigmatized sex often needed to dull their inhibitions. In *Cherry Grove,* her wonderfully evocative history of the gay Fire Island resort, Esther Newton writes that for many homosexuals, sex was possible only under the heavy fog of drink. "It is no exaggeration to say," she writes of Cherry Grove in the 1940s, that "alcohol was the lifeblood of Grove social life and that drunkenness was not only accepted but conferred status." She quotes one Grove resident as saying, "Until you had fallen off the boardwalk you were not really a Cherry Grover."[7] Pre-Stonewall clinical studies show extremely high rates of alcohol consumption among gay men, while later studies of gay men drawn from more representative samples in the seventies present conflicting results: Some indicate that one third of gay men had problems with alcohol and that gays were twice as likely as straights to be alcoholics. Others have found fewer differences between heterosexuals and homosexuals in alcohol consumption and abuse.[8]

Some investigators now believe that the prevalence of concurrency amplified transmission among gay men by factors of 10 to 100 times.

Since gay liberation coincided with a steep rise in society's use of recreational drugs generally, it is no surprise that the gay world had an active drug subculture. The most sexually active urban gay men tended to consume large amounts of recreational drugs, including cocaine, marijuana, THC, MDA, LSD, and speed. The party circuits in the gay resorts of both coasts were famous for their open use of drugs, and the literature of the era is filled with romanticized depictions of drug use as an integral part of the gay male experience.

Gay life even had its own favorite drugs, the most ubiquitous being nitrate inhalants, or "poppers." Poppers were initially manufactured as treatments for angina pectoris, a painful heart condition. But they also produce a momentarily powerful "rush" that dilutes blood vessels and, for many, enhances sexual pleasure and prolongs orgasm. They also relax muscles, including the sphincter muscle, making them an aid to both anal sex and fisting. Poppers became so popular in urban gay circles in the seventies that popper manufacturers rivaled bathhouse owners as the biggest advertisers in the gay press. A CDC study during the early eighties showed that 85 percent of gay men used poppers, compared to only 15 percent of heterosexual men, making poppers the closest thing we had to a truly gay drug. Poppers became so ubiquitous in the urban gay world that many investigators long suspected that AIDS was caused by poppers. Since poppers have been shown to have an adverse effect on the immune system, they may have played a significant role in making people more susceptible to HIV infection.

A significant subset of gay men straddled the line between the gay community and the world of injection drug users (IDUs). Since injection drugs had created a parallel HIV epidemic among IDUs, this intersection between gay men and IDUs created a viral "bridge" that linked the two epidemics. Of the first 1,000 AIDS cases, for example, 642 were gay men and 154 were injection drug users, but an additional 81 were both: gay male IDUs. (By contrast, only 1 out of the 54 Haitians and none of the 7 hemophiliacs in the original cohort of 1,000 were also IDUs). There has been much speculation on the significance of this connection, a linkage between the two most intense pools of infection that continues to this day.[9]

Travel

Still another factor contributing to rapid dissemination was widespread travel and mobility. This affected the health of the whole world by making possible the rapid spread of new diseases from isolated pockets to great urban centers and from one urban center to another.[10] As a glance at the travel ads of any major gay publication will attest, many gay men love to travel, and few populations in history have been as mobile. Sexual vacations to Third World countries with thriving sex industries, such as Haiti and Thailand, were very popular in the seventies. Within the United States a party circuit evolved—called simply the Circuit—that found men gathering several times per year for huge, nationally known megaparties that often lasted several days. In some sense the gay meccas of L.A. and New York and San Francisco became one large, interconnected bicoastal community during the seventies, a community in which well-heeled travelers intermingled sexually as well as socially. The importance of this factor was highlighted at the very outset of the epidemic, when researchers discovered clusters of gay men in New York, San Francisco, and Los Angeles who were connected to each other through sexual relations. Patient Zero, the airline steward made notorious by Randy Shilts in *And the Band Played On* (not because he was thought first to introduce HIV to North America, as sometimes erroneously reported, but because his mobility and sexual activity placed him at the center of several important clusters of early AIDS cases), was only one among thousands of highly mobile gay men who helped transport HIV quickly and efficiently.

Increased virulence

According to a theory advanced by Amherst biologist Paul Ewald in his 1993 book *Evolution of Infectious Disease,* the high levels of HIV transmission among gay men and intravenous (IV) drug users may have led to the evolution of new strains of more virulent and infectious HIV. Viral infectiousness is defined as the ability of a virus to enter and infect a cell in the target host. Virulence describes the ability of that virus to replicate within that cell, in the process disrupting the cell's natural function and causing illness. According to the theory of natural selection, which operates with the same relentless logic among viruses as among elephants, only those viral strains best suited to their environment will survive and be passed along. When people had relatively few sex partners and might spend many years with the same person, the only strains of HIV likely to survive and be passed along were those that delayed causing illness for long enough to give their relatively monogamous hosts a chance to have sexual relations with other partners and pass the strain along. In other words, only those strains so mild that they allowed their hosts decades of healthy life were likely to survive in a relatively monogamous world. More virulent strains would cause their hosts to fall ill and stop having sex relatively quickly, before they could find additional partners, and so those more virulent strains would generally die with their hosts.

> *From the virus's point of view, the ecology of liberation was a royal road to adaptive triumph.*

When HIV entered communities characterized by large numbers of concurrent partners, however, the virus no longer had to reside in the same person for decades in order to be passed along. As a result, whenever a random mutation of a highly virulent strain arose that also had a high degree of infectiousness, it now had a distinct advantage. Since it was more aggressive, it was more likely to be passed along in any given sexual encounter. And since its more promiscuous host was likely to have many partners in the few years before becoming ill, it had ample opportunity to be passed along. Thus, the logic of natural selection ceased favoring the extremely mild strains and now increasingly favored the most aggressive ones.

The core and the bridge

STD epidemics often begin in small cores of people who suffer from multiple risk factors. This phenomenon was observed among gay men from the very beginning of the epidemic. In 1983 leading AIDS doctor Joseph Sonnabend wrote in an influential article that "it appears that the disease has been occurring in a rather small subset [of gay men] characterized by having had sexual contact with large numbers of different partners in settings where the carriage of CMV [cytomegalovirus] in particular (but also of other sexually transmitted infections) is high." He attributed this to the "unprecedented level of promiscuity" within this subset.[11] A few years later PWA activist Michael Callen would not feel any need to elaborate his statement that "unwittingly, and with the best of revolutionary intentions, a small subset of gay men managed to create disease settings equivalent to those of poor third-world nations," thereby facilitating the explosion of AIDS. Even within gay urban circles and even among activists, AIDS was thought of as a disease of the promiscuous. And, at first, it probably was.

In the late eighties Professor James Thompson, chairman of the department of statistics at Rice University, published statistical models that calculated what would happen to the incidence of HIV in gay populations with and without such core groups. His work indicated that the overall level of sexual interaction that characterized most gay men was not sufficient to push HIV over the epidemic threshold in most communities, but that the extraordinarily high levels of activity that characterized a subset of the gay population made epidemic amplification inevitable. In perhaps his most startling and disturbing model, Thompson created two scenarios. In one, a theoretical gay population has a uniform sexual rate of 30 contacts per month. In the other, the total number of contacts within the population remains the same, but most sexual activity is shifted to the core, so that 10 percent of the population has 150 contacts per month and the other 90 percent has only a few contacts. Thompson showed that despite the fact that this second population has the same total number of contacts as the first, the fact that most of the contacts have been shifted to the core has the same effect as if the entire group had doubled its number of contacts. In other words, the same number of contacts produces twice as much new infection if those contacts are concentrated among a small core of men. Thompson's models, which are rarely discussed in gay prevention circles, are unambiguous. It is not anything particular about homosexuality that renders AIDS possible in the gay population, Thompson wrote. "It is the presence of extraordinarily sexually active individuals in the homosexual community which causes the problem. . . . It should be pointed out to the gay community that even if most of the members of the community cut down on their activity and/or practice 'safe sex,' even the less promiscuous are seriously endangered by a small, highly promiscuous sub-group."[12]

Bridging

In many societies, however, small subsets of people can be burdened with high levels of sexually transmitted diseases without contributing to a wider epidemic. The factor that most often prevents a disease from bridging from a core to the rest of the population is, quite baldly, prejudice and stigma. People in cores tend to be members of poor, oppressed minorities who are often marginalized and visibly ill—and therefore often shunned as sexual partners by the majority. In the gay world, however, almost the opposite was the case. There was no prejudice or stigma directed against the A-list: beautiful, well-heeled men who were both the most sexually active and the most desirable. Virtually no one stigmatized their behavior. Indeed, many people felt the behavior of A-list gay men represented the apex of gay liberation, something to be envied and emulated rather than shunned. And among the majority who did not participate in the extremes of the gay fast lane, there was very little or no stigma against having affairs or brief encounters with those who did. The seventies and early eighties were, after all, a relaxed era in which many gay men—including many in relationships—prided themselves on being more open-minded and tolerant about the occasional tryst than heterosexuals. As a result, there appears to have been a tremendous amount of sexual mixing between the most highly active (and infected) gay men and the rest of the population. Men who had only one extracurricular partner a year mixed freely with those who had hundreds. Someone involved in a long-term relationship in which he himself chose to remain monogamous might often assume, or know for certain, that his lover had dalliances with other casual partners, sometimes lots of them. Because of this, any disease agent becoming endemic within the sexual core of gay men had ample opportunity to radiate out efficiently through the rest of the gay population.

Our collective gay response to AIDS has never included a sober evaluation of the ways the sexual culture of the seventies produced the AIDS epidemic.

This kind of mixing happened throughout the gay landscape and was facilitated by all sorts of institutions, but some experts believe that bathhouses played a particularly crucial role in this process. In the first place, the virus took advantage of the baths to exploit the fact that people with HIV tend to be highly infectious for a couple of months right after they become infected themselves. What likely occurred (on a massive scale) is that a regular bath-goer would become infected one night at the tubs and then, during the next couple of months when he was extremely likely to transmit infection, would return many times and have perhaps dozens of partners, infecting several. Many of those partners would also frequent bathhouses and they would repeat the process, primarily using the medium of baths and sex clubs to accumulate large numbers of partners in the limited window of maximum transmission. While those who habituated baths quickly became saturated with HIV, there were tens of thousands of additional men who went to the baths much less often—from once every few weeks to once a year or less. These men were spread out all along the behavioral continuum. Some might even be in fairly monogamous relationships, for whom the baths were simply an occasional treat. But once there, they ran a high likelihood of having sex with the very people whom, from a biological standpoint, they most needed to avoid. So it appears that the baths both created the conditions for the most sexually active core to become quickly infected, and then created the ideal conditions to bridge the resultant epidemic rapidly across the gay landscape.

Some researchers now believe that under these conditions HIV spread almost like measles or chicken pox in its original, explosive phase in the early eighties. It has been estimated that in the early eighties the average infected gay man infected an average of five additional gay men. Such a mind-boggling reproductive rate for a virus that's relatively difficult to transmit would require several conditions: that infected men had very large numbers of partners, that they engaged in the most transmitting form of fluid exchange, and that they had those partners in quick succession, during the brief initial period of high infectiousness at the outset of their own infection. Commercial sex establishments are obviously not the only ways that people can engage in such behavior, especially in urban populations where much of social life centered around cruising and bars. But bathhouses and sex clubs clearly fulfilled those conditions in extraordinarily efficient ways, causing some researchers to believe that they played the vital role that schools and movie theaters play for diseases like measles and chicken pox. A 1989 epidemiological survey of AIDS transmission in the gay world noted that "gay bath houses and sex clubs functioned for gay men in the same way that 'shooting galleries' have functioned for drug injectors in establishing the AIDS epidemic and the spread of HIV infection."[13]

Understanding the role of core groups is hardly just an academic exercise. Because of core groups' concentration and their ability to spread infection both inside and outside the core, they make logical targets for prevention programs. In the early nineties researchers created models to examine what might happen to the future number of infections if public health officials prevented 100 new infections today within a core, as opposed to preventing 100 new infections outside the core. One study indicated that within ten years a "policy of targeting the one-time intervention at the core averts *ten times as many cases* as would have been averted by a policy directed at the noncore." If, for example, 100 cases of gonorrhea are prevented in a noncore today, that would prevent an additional 426 cases within ten years. But preventing 100 cases of gonorrhea within a core prevents an additional 4,278 cases. Approximately the same numbers apply to HIV. Preventing 100 cases in a noncore today, the study reported, prevents an additional 201 cases in ten years, while preventing 100 cases within a core prevents an additional 2,106 cases.

All these factors are central to gay life

"It was an historic accident that HIV disease first manifested itself in the gay populations of the east and west coasts of the United States," wrote British sociologist Jeffrey Weeks in *AIDS and Contemporary History* in 1993.[14] His opinion has been almost universal among gay and AIDS activists even to this day. Yet there is little "accidental" about the sexual ecology described above. Multiple concurrent partners, versatile anal sex, core group behavior centered in commercial sex establishments, widespread recreational drug abuse, repeated waves of STDs and constant intake of antibiotics, sexual tourism and travel—these factors were not "accidents." Multipartner anal sex was encouraged, celebrated, considered a central component of liberation. Core group behavior in baths and sex clubs was deemed by many the quintessence of freedom. Versatility was declared a political imperative. Analingus was pronounced the champagne of gay sex, a palpable gesture of revolution. STDs were to be worn like badges of honor, antibiotics to be taken with pride.

Far from being accidents, these things characterized the very foundation of what it supposedly meant to experience gay liberation. Taken together they formed a sexual ecology of almost incalculably catastrophic dimensions, a classic feedback loop in which virtually every factor served to amplify every other. From the virus's point of view, the ecology of liberation was a royal road to adaptive triumph. From many gay men's point of view, it proved a trapdoor to hell on earth.

It would be reassuring to say that in the epidemic's second decade all of this has become common knowledge, that AIDS prevention is now grounded in a frank and full understanding of the ecological principles briefly sketched here, principles learned painfully with much death and loss. But sadly for gay men, that is not the case. Our collective gay response to AIDS has never included a sober evaluation of the ways the sexual culture of the seventies produced the AIDS epidemic. Quite the opposite. The enterprise of AIDS prevention in the gay world has strenuously avoided any detailed examination of these mechanisms. Their very discussion is considered offensive, homophobic, self-loathing. Instead, we have sought to minimize or even deny these factors, partly in order to preserve as much as possible the gains of the gay sexual revolution—the very "gains" that brought us AIDS.

Notes

1. Michael Callen, "Dinosaur's Diary," *QW* magazine, July 26, 1991.

2. David F. Greenberg, *The Construction of Homosexuality* (The University of Chicago Press, 1988), p. 26.

3. Carl Wittman, "A Gay Manifesto," reprinted in *Out of the Closets: Voices of Gay Liberation* (Douglas, 1972), p. 337.

4. For a discussion of the effects of versatility, see D. Trichopoulos, L. Spiros, and E. Petridou, "Homosexual Role Separation and the Spread of AIDS," *Lancet 2* (1988), p. 966.

5. The most thorough discussion of the difference between serial and concurrent multiple partners is contained in an unpublished paper by Martina Morris, Columbia University.

6. One study by Dr. Ann C. Collier of the University of Washington in Seattle found HIV in the semen of 22 percent of HIV-infected subjects but could find no predictors of who would be shedding virus.

7. Esther Newton, *Cherry Grove, Fire Island: Sixty Years in America's First Gay and Lesbian Town* (Beacon Press, 1993), p. 78.

8. Duncan Osborne, *Outweek* magazine 77, p. 38.

9. Ann Guidici Fettner and William A Check, *The Truth About AIDS* (Holt, Rinehart and Winston, 1984), p. 69.

10. Laurie Garrett, *The Coming Plague* (Farrar, Strauss and Giroux, 1994), p. 653.

11. J.A. Sonnabend, "The Etiology of AIDS," *AIDS Research* 1:1 (1983), pp. 2–3.

12. J. R. Thompson, "AIDS: The Mismanagement of an Epidemic," *Computer Math Applications*, Vol. 18, No. 10/11 (1989), pp. 965–72. Thompson's quote is from *The Houston Chronicle*, July 14, 1987.

13. Jonathan M. Mann, ed., *AIDS in the World: A Global Report* (Harvard University Press, 1992), p. 185.

14. Berridge and Strong, eds., *AIDS and Contemporary History* (Cambridge University Press, 1993), p. 23.

12

Gay Men Can Have Safe Sex and Avoid AIDS

Joseph Sonnabend and Richard Berkowitz

Joseph Sonnabend is a physician who treats victims of HIV/AIDS. Richard Berkowitz is an AIDS activist who cowrote the 1983 pamphlet "How to Have Sex in an Epidemic," one of the first published articles to advocate safe sex and condom use to prevent AIDS.

In his controversial 1997 book *Sexual Ecology: AIDS and the Destiny of Gay Men*, Gabriel Rotello wrote that promiscuous sexual practices of gay men in the 1970s and 1980s furthered the spread of AIDS. Rotello concluded that gay men cannot use condoms and practice safe sex with enough consistency to prevent a "second wave" of AIDS, and he called for gay men to embrace sexual restraint and monogamy. However, a closer examination of the health data indicates that the rate of infection of HIV and other sexually transmitted diseases is falling—indicating that safe sex works to prevent disease. Moreover, stressing sexual restraint as the solution risks a return to the days when all gay sex was condemned by society and repressed within the gay population. Society should respect diversity in sexual expression and should redouble its efforts to teach methods of safe sex to prevent AIDS.

*S*exual Ecology must be commended for its accurate analysis of how widespread changes in sexual behavior among gay men in the '70s propelled the spread of AIDS. Hopefully, [the book's author] Gabriel Rotello won't be maligned for publicizing this as we were (with Michael Callen) in 1981; back then, the gay leadership that had unwittingly encouraged the very behaviors that led to this tragedy dismissed any suggestion that lifestyle played a role in AIDS. Like Rotello, we pointed out the health risks in a way of life that promoted the spread of STDS, before the invention of safe sex. It's on this issue of safe sex that we part. Rotello believes gay men cannot practice safe sex consistently enough to prevent a second wave of AIDS, and essentially calls for the end of promiscuity. In 1981, we agreed. But now that safe sex has been shown to work, we believe the most im-

Reprinted from Joseph Sonnabend and Richard Berkowitz, "A Second Look," *POZ*, June 1997, © POZ Publishing L.L.C., with permission. For *POZ* subscriptions, call 800-973-2376.

portant task is to encourage gay men who are at risk to practice it.

The prospect of a second wave gives *Sexual Ecology* its urgency. While there is little hard evidence to support such a disaster, the possibility should force us to redouble our efforts to keep sex safe. According to Dr. Thomas Coates, director of the University of California at San Francisco's AIDS Research Institute, new HIV infections in San Francisco fell to an estimated 650 in 1994 from a high of 8,000 in 1982. He attributes this dramatic reduction to community-based HIV prevention programs targeted to gay men. The rates of rectal gonorrhea—the best indicator of highest-risk sex—remain at all-time lows nationwide. In 1982; some 2,000 cases were reported in New York City; in 1995, there were fewer than 30. San Francisco reported around 5,000 cases in 1982; 1994 saw fewer than 80. Rotello cites a study indicating an "alarming" increase in rectal gonorrhea in Washington state in 1989. Had he checked rates after 1989, he would have found a continuous decline; changes in one year cannot indicate a steady trend. Even when Rotello acknowledges this decline, he contends that because rectal gonorrhea is curable, falling rates do not argue against a second wave. If there was a second wave by the early '90s, surely we'd be seeing increases in rectal gonorrhea—and we are not.

In practice, safer sex has included oral sex without condoms (and without ejaculation), and while risk to an individual cannot be excluded, safe sex has curtailed the epidemic. We must therefore continue to emphasize the need for safe sex; this may now be easier as it is finally admitted that AIDS will not become a heterosexual epidemic. Hopefully, the vast amounts Or money wasted on nontargeted campaigns like "America Responds to AIDS" and educating non-IV-drug-using heterosexual men at very little risk can now be directed toward gay men (particularly young gay men), women at risk and needle-exchange programs.

Safe sex has been shown to work.

Rotello cites a study showing that the reduction in unsafe sex in the late '80s, if sustained, could "reduce . . . the rate of HIV infections below the epidemic threshold"; however, if unsafe sex rises by even a very small amount, HIV transmissions would persist at epidemic levels. One has two choices in response to this. Rotello urges the gay community to establish institutions that reward sexual restraint, monogamy and marriage. On the other hand, we can use this information to continually instruct gay men on the crucial importance of safe sex. If we choose Rotello's prescription, it had better work: Otherwise we'll be in worse trouble because of the deemphasis of safe sex implicit in the message that it hasn't worked. Attempts to modify sexual behavior at the level called for by Rotello have been notoriously unsuccessful. There is an inherent danger in Rotello's proposals to forestall future infections. For those for whom monogamy and sexual restraint are unworkable, the failure to respect the diversity of sexual expression will doom them to a life of shame, guilt and AIDS.

Sex is one of life's joys and central to one's being. We shouldn't allow ourselves to return to the miserable repressions that once ruined so many lives. For example, a Canadian study found that among all young men 18 to 27, gay and straight, those who are celibate are far more likely to try to harm or kill themselves than those who are sexually active; the highest rate was in celibate gay male youth. Could it be that the same old inhibitions, meanness and conservative influences drive the new Puritanism hiding behind *Sexual Ecology's* facade of concern for the future health of gay men? AIDS is a terrible reality, and sex can no longer be as free as it once was. But in encouraging safety, we must also make it clear that the need to modify certain behaviors is not an attack on sex.

Organizations to Contact

The editors have compiled the following list of organizations concerned with the issues debated in this book. The descriptions are derived from materials provided by the organizations. All have publications or information available for interested readers. The list was compiled on the date of publication of the present volume; the information provided here may change. Be aware that many organizations take several weeks or longer to respond to inquiries, so allow as much time as possible.

Advocates for Youth
1025 Vermont Ave. NW, Suite 200, Washington, DC 20005
(202) 347-5700 • fax: (202) 347-2263
e-mail: info@advocatesforyouth.org
website: http://www.advocatesforyouth.org

Advocates for Youth supports programs that increase youths' opportunities and abilities to make healthy decisions about sexuality. It publishes the newsletters *Passages* and *Transitions* as well as fact sheets on STDs and AIDS.

AIDS Coalition to Unleash Power (ACT UP)
332 Bleecker St., G5, New York, NY 10014
(212) 966-4873
e-mail: actupny@panix.com • website: http://www.actupny.org

ACT UP is a group of individuals committed to direct action to end the AIDS crisis. Through education and demonstrations, ACT UP fights against discrimination and for adequate funding for AIDS research, health care, and housing for people with AIDS. It also supports the dissemination of information about safer sex, clean needles, and other AIDS prevention. ACT UP publishes action manuals, such as *Time to Become an AIDS Activist*, and on-line action reports.

The Alan Guttmacher Institute
120 Wall St., New York, NY 10005
(212) 248-1111 • fax: (212) 248-1951
e-mail: info@agi-usa.org • website: http://www.agi-usa.org

The institute works to protect and expand the reproductive choices of all women and men. It strives to ensure people's access to the information and services they need to exercise their rights and responsibilities concerning sexual activity, reproduction, and family planning. Among the institute's publications are the books *Teenage Pregnancy in Industrialized Countries* and *Today's Adolescents, Tomorrow's Parents: A Portrait of the Americas* and the report *Sex and America's Teenagers*.

American Civil Liberties Union (ACLU)
125 Broad St., 18th Fl., New York, NY 10004-2400
(212) 549-2500
e-mail: aclu@aclu.org • website: http://www.aclu.org

The ACLU is a national organization that works to defend Americans' civil rights guaranteed by the U.S. Constitution. The ACLU's Lesbian and Gay Rights/AIDS Project handles litigation, education, and public policy work on behalf of gays and lesbians. It publishes the semiannual newsletter *Civil Liberties Alert* as well as policy papers such as "AIDS and Civil Liberties."

American Foundation for AIDS Research (AmFAR)
120 Wall St., 13th Fl., New York, NY 10005
(212) 806-1600 • fax: (212) 806-1601
e-mail: webmaster@amfar.org • website: http://www.amfar.org

AmFAR supports AIDS prevention and research and advocates AIDS-related public policy. It publishes several monographs, compendiums, journals, and periodic publications, including the *AIDS/HIV Treatment Directory*, published twice a year; the newsletter *HIV/AIDS Educator and Reporter*, published three times a year; and the quarterly *AmFAR* newsletter.

American Social Health Association (ASHA)
PO Box 13827, Research Triangle Park, NC 27709
(919) 361-8400 • fax: (919) 361-8425
Herpes hot line: (919) 361-8488
website: http://www.ashastd.org

ASHA is a nonprofit organization dedicated to stopping sexually transmitted diseases and their harmful consequences. It advocates increased federal funding for STD programs and sound public policies on STD control. The association distributes the quarterly newsletter *STD News* and maintains an on-line sexual health glossary, and its Herpes Resource Center publishes the quarterly newsletter the *Helper*. ASHA's Women's Health Program provides information on pelvic inflammatory disease, vaginitis, Pap tests, and the effects of herpes simplex and HIV testing on pregnancy.

Center for AIDS Prevention Studies
University of California, San Francisco
74 New Montgomery, Suite 600, San Francisco, CA 94105
(415) 597-9100 • fax: (415) 597-9213
website: http:// www.caps.ucsf.edu

The center is committed to the prevention of HIV and AIDS. It sponsors research on the risk factors for AIDS and publishes a newsletter, fact sheets, and press releases.

Centers for Disease Control and Prevention (CDC)
Center for HIV, STD, and TB Prevention (CHSTP)
1600 Clifton Rd. NE, Atlanta, GA 30333
(888) CDC-FACT (232-3228) • fax: (888) CDC-FAXX (232-3299)
National STD hot line: (800) 227-8922
e-mail: NCHSTP@cdc.gov
website: http://www.cdc.gov/nchstp/od/nchstp.html

The CDC is the government agency charged with protecting the public health of the nation by preventing and controlling diseases and by responding to public health emergencies. The CHSTP, a program of the CDC, publishes fact sheets on STDs and the *HIV/AIDS Prevention Newsletter*.

Citizens Alliance for VD Awareness (CAVDA)
PO Box 31915, Chicago, IL 60631-0915
(847) 398-3378 • fax: (847) 398-7309

CAVDA is a not-for-profit organization that produces informational and educational products for use within the disciplines of STD and AIDS control. The alliance also publishes a quarterly newsletter, *STD Spotlight.*

Family Health International (FHI)
PO Box 13950, Research Triangle Park, NC 27709
(919) 544-7040 • fax: (919) 544-7261
website: http://www.fhi.org

FHI is a not-for-profit organization committed to helping women and men have access to safe, effective, acceptable, and affordable family planning methods; preventing the spread of AIDS and other sexually transmitted diseases; and improving the health of women and children. Its AIDS Control and Prevention Project publishes an annual report and the book *Control of Sexually Transmitted Diseases: A Handbook for the Design and Management of Programs.*

HIV/AIDS Treatment Information Service (ATIS)
PO Box 6303, Rockville, MD 20849-6303
(800) HIV-0440 (448-0440) • fax: (301) 519-6616
e-mail: atis@hivatis.org • website: http://www.hivatis.org

ATIS provides information about federally approved treatment guidelines for HIV and AIDS. It publishes *Principles of Therapy of HIV Infection* as well as reports and guidelines for treating HIV infection in adults, adolescents, and children.

Kaiser Family Foundation
2400 Sand Hill Rd., Menlo Park, CA 94025
(650) 854-9400 • fax: (650) 854-4800
website: http://www.kff.org

The foundation is an independent health care philanthropy concerned with reproductive health and the spread of STDs. It publishes the reports *Sex Education in the Schools, The Demography of Sexual Behavior, 1997 National Survey of Americans on AIDS/HIV,* and daily on-line health reports.

National AIDS Fund
1400 I St. NW, Suite 1220, Washington, DC 20005
(202) 408-4848 • fax: (202) 408-1818
e-mail: info@aidsfund.org • website: http://www.aidsfund.org

The fund seeks to eliminate AIDS as a major health and social problem. Its members work in partnership with the public and private sectors to provide care and to prevent new infections by means of advocacy, grants, research, and education. The fund publishes the monthly newsletter *News from the National AIDS Fund.*

National Institute of Allergy and Infectious Diseases (NIAID)
Office of Communications
Building 31, Room 7A-50
31 Center Dr., MSC 2520, Bethesda, MD 20892-2520
e-mail: ocpostoffice@flash.niaid.nih.gov • website: http://www.niaid.nih.gov

NIAID is the program of the National Institutes of Health that deals with AIDS and sexually transmitted diseases. The institute conducts and supports research on diagnostic tests, treatments, and vaccines, and carries out epidemiological studies. It publishes a monthly newsletter, information on its research activities, and many informational publications, including *Sexually Transmitted Diseases: An Introduction* and *HIV and Adolescents.*

Planned Parenthood Federation of America
810 Seventh Ave., New York, NY 10019
(212) 541-7800 • fax: (212) 245-1845
e-mail: communications@ppfa.org
website: http://www.plannedparenthood.org

Planned Parenthood believes that all individuals should have access to comprehensive sexuality education in order to make decisions about their own fertility. It publishes information on protecting against STDs and AIDS.

Bibliography

Books

Michael W. Adler   *ABC of Sexually Transmitted Diseases.* London: BMJ, 1995.

Allan M. Brandt   *No Magic Bullet: A Social History of Venereal Disease in the United States Since 1880.* New York: Oxford University Press, 1987.

Elinor Burkett   *The Gravest Show on Earth: America in the Age of AIDS.* Boston: Houghton Mifflin, 1995.

Ralph J. DiClemente and John L. Peterson, eds.   *Preventing AIDS: Theories and Methods of Behavioral Interventions.* New York: Plenum, 1994.

Thomas R. Eng and William T. Butler, eds.   *The Hidden Epidemic: Confronting Sexually Transmitted Diseases.* Washington, DC: National Academy Press, 1996.

Lawrence O. Gostin and Zita Lazzarini   *Human Rights and Public Health in the AIDS Pandemic.* New York: Oxford University Press, 1997.

Gilbert Herdt, ed.   *Sexual Cultures and Migration in the Era of AIDS: Anthropological and Demographic Perspectives.* New York: Oxford University Press, 1997.

King K. Holmes et al.   *Sexually Transmitted Diseases.* New York: McGraw-Hill, 1998.

Earvin Johnson   *What You Can Do to Avoid AIDS.* New York: Times Books, 1996.

Jacob Lipman   *Soap, Water, and Sex: A Lively Guide to the Benefits of Sexual Hygiene and to Coping with Sexually Transmitted Diseases.* Amherst, NY: Prometheus Books, 1998.

Joe S. McIlhaney and Marion McIlhaney   *Sex: What You Don't Know Can Kill You.* Grand Rapids, MI: Baker Books, 1997.

Susan Moore, Doreen Rosenthal, and Anne Mitchell   *Youth, AIDS, and Sexually Transmitted Diseases.* New York: Routledge, 1997.

Cindy Patton   *Fatal Advice: How Safe-Sex Education Went Wrong.* Durham, NC: Duke University Press, 1996.

Gabriel Rotello   *Sexual Ecology: AIDS and the Destiny of Gay Men.* New York: Dutton, 1997.

Mark S. Senak   *HIV, AIDS, and the Law: A Guide to Our Rights and Challenges.* New York: Insight Books, 1996.

Ben Sonder   *Epidemic of Silence: The Facts About Women and AIDS.* Danbury, CT: Franklin Watts, 1995.

Lawrence R. Stanberry   *Understanding Herpes.* Jackson: University Press of Mississippi, 1998.

Samuel G. Woods   *Everything You Need to Know About STD: Sexually Transmitted Disease.* New York: Rosen, 1997.

Periodicals

Richard Berkowitz   "Before the Revolution," *POZ*, June 1997. Available from LLC, 349 W. Twelfth St., New York, NY 10014-1721.

Tim Bergling   "Riders on the Storm," *Genre*, October 1997. Available from Box 18449, Anaheim, CA 92817-8449.

Shannon Brownlee, Marci McDonald, and Elise Hackerman   "AIDS Comes to Small Town America," *U.S. News & World Report*, November 10, 1997.

Chandler Burr   "The AIDS Exception: Privacy vs. Public Health," *Atlantic Monthly*, June 1997.

Betsy Carpenter   "The Other Epidemic: Genital Herpes Rages Among Women and Devastates Some Newborns," *U.S. News & World Report*, November 10, 1997.

Stephanie A. Crockett   "Doing It to Death," *Essence*, July 1997.

Mubarak S. Dahir   "Name Calling," *Advocate*, February 17, 1998.

Meghan Daum   "Safe-Sex Lies," *New York Times Magazine*, January 21, 1996.

Patricia Donovan   "Confronting a Hidden Epidemic: The Institute of Medicine's Report on Sexually Transmitted Diseases," *Family Planning Perspectives*, March/April 1997. Available from 120 Wall St., New York, NY 10005.

Mac Edwards   "Secrecy Surrounding Sexuality Hinders STD-Prevention Programs," *SIECUS Report*, February/March 1997. Available from 130 W. 142nd St., Suite 350, New York, NY 10036-7802.

Anna Forbes   "'Names' Versus 'Unique Identifiers': The 'How' of HIV Case Reporting," *SIECUS Report*, February/March 1998.

Glen Freyer   "Men and Safe Sex: How Careful Are They?" *Glamour*, May 1996.

Jesse Green   "Flirting with Suicide," *New York Times Magazine*, September 15, 1996.

Lawrence O. Gostin et al.   "National HIV Case Reporting for the United States," *New England Journal of Medicine*, October 16, 1997. Available from 10 Shattuck St., Boston, MA 02115-6094.

Russell W. Gough   "Does Abstinence Education Work?" *World & I*, August 1997. Available from 3600 New York Ave. NE, Washington, DC 20002.

Maggie Hadleigh-West   "Safe Sex," *Ms.*, March/April 1996.

Carolyn P. Hagan   "STDs: What Not to Worry About," *Mademoiselle*, September 1994.

Karen Houppert   "Risky Sex," *Glamour*, August 1997.

Anne M. Johnson   "Condoms and HIV Transmission," *New England Journal of Medicine*, August 11, 1994.

William B. Kaliher   "How Federal and State Policies Spread AIDS," *World & I*, May 1998.

Leslie Laurence   "How Ob-Gyns Are Failing Women," *Glamour*, October 1997.

Cindi Leive   "The Night the Condom Broke," *Glamour*, May 1995.

Rodger McFarlane   "Painful Truths," *POZ*, June 1997.

Martina Morris, Jane Zavisca, and Laura Dean   "Social and Sexual Networks: Their Role in the Spread of HIV/AIDS Among Young Gay Men," *AIDS Education and Prevention*, vol. 7, 1995. Available from Guilford Publications, 72 Spring St., New York, NY 10012.

Richard Nadler   "Abstaining from Sex Education," *National Review*, September 15, 1997.

Kristine Napier   "Chastity Programs Shatter Sex-Ed Myths," *Policy Review*, May/June 1997.

Tamar Nordenberg   "Condoms: Barriers to Bad News," *FDA Consumer*, March/April 1998.

Walt Odets   "The Fatal Mistakes of AIDS Education," *Harper's*, May 1995.

Marc Peyser   "A Deadly Dance," *Newsweek*, September 29, 1997.

Roger A. Roffman et al.   "Relapse Prevention as an Intervention Model for HIV Risk Reduction in Gay and Bisexual Men," *AIDS Education and Prevention*, February 1998.

Gabriel Rotello   "No One Left to Track," *Advocate*, April 14, 1998.

Rita Rubin   "Gay Bathhouses, Now with a Mission," *U.S. News & World Report*, October 7, 1996.

John S. Santelli et al.   "The Use of Condoms with Other Contraceptive Methods Among Young Men and Women," *Family Planning Perspectives*, November/December 1997.

Mark Schoofs   "Who's Afraid of Reinfection?" *POZ*, May 1997.

Jessica Shaw   "Let's Talk About (Safe) Sex," *Seventeen*, March 1998.

SIECUS Report   "Sexually Transmitted Diseases," February/March 1997.

Sheryl Gay Stolberg   "U.S. Awakes to Epidemic of Sexual Diseases," *New York Times*, March 9, 1998.

Jeff Stryker   "Abstinence or Else!" *Nation*, June 16, 1997.

USA Today   "Detecting Sexually Transmitted Diseases," October 1997.

Bernard A. Weisberger   "The Persistence of the Serpent," *American Heritage*, November 1994.

Philip Yam   "Dangerous Sex," *Scientific American*, February 1995.

Index

abstinence
  until marriage is unrealistic, 33, 38
  works for some teens, 39
African Americans, 10
  HIV testing among, 62
  women, 47
AIDS
  cases in U.S. vs. Cuba, 53
  control efforts must protect civil
    rights, 57
    con, 49
  legal protections for patients are weak,
    59
  promiscuity among gay men
    contributed to epidemics, 70
  and public health policies, 50–51,
    59–60
  safe sex among gay men can prevent,
    83
  see also HIV
AIDS and Contemporary History (Weeks),
  81
AIDS Prevention Act of 1997 (proposed),
  49, 51
alcohol. *See* substance abuse
American Civil Liberties Union, 57
Americans with Disabilities Act, 60
anal sex, 70–71, 81
And the Band Played On (Shilts), 77

Bayer, Ron, 50
Berkowitz, Richard, 83
birth control
  most does not prevent STDs, 18
body fluids
  avoidance of, in safer sex, 14
  women's, human papillomavirus in,
    25
Bragdon v. Abbot, 64
Burkett, Elinor, 54
Burr, Chandler, 49

Callen, Michael, 71, 78, 83
Center for AIDS Prevention Studies, 32
Centers for Disease Control (CDC)
  AIDS control efforts by, 50
  on HIV infection in U.S., 54
  tracking of STDs by, is inadequate,
    46–47
Cherry Grove (Newton), 76
chlamydia, 8, 18, 45

  in semen, 24
civil rights, 49
Coates, Thomas, 55, 84
Coburn, Tom, 49, 51, 56
condoms
  are best protection for intercourse, 18
  distribution of to teens promotes sex,
    40
  female, 18
  in HIV prevention, have failed, 54, 55
  how to use, 18
The Construction of Homosexuality
  (Greenberg), 72
Cuba
  treatment of AIDS patients in, 50,
    52–53
  results of, 53–55

Darling, Juanita, 50
Dorland's Medical Dictionary, 23
drugs. *See* intravenous drug users;
  substance abuse

Elders, M. Joycelyn, 22, 37
Evolution of Infectious Disease (Ewald), 77
Ewald, Paul, 77

Fertility and Sterility, 24

"A Gay Manifesto" (Wittman), 72
gay men
  promiscuity among contributed to
    AIDS epidemic, 70–82
  reporting names of, will discourage
    HIV testing, 62
  safe sex among, can prevent AIDS,
    83–85
  teenage, sex education should be
    relevant to, 33
Genitourinary Medicine, 23
gonorrhea, 8, 18
  disproportionate funding for, 46
*The Gravest Show on Earth: America in the
  Age of AIDS* (Burkett), 54
Greenberg, David, 72
*Guidelines for Comprehensive Sexuality
  Education* (SIECUS), 25–26

Hartigan, John D., 40
health insurance, 11
Hepatitis C virus, 24

herpes, 8
  prevalence of, 46
*Hidden Epidemic: Confronting Sexually
  Transmitted Diseases* (Institute of
  Medicine Committee on Prevention
  and Control of STDs), 11
HIV (human immunodeficiency virus)
  among youth, 37–38
  condoms do not prevent spread of, 41
  and name reporting, 57
    will set back public health efforts, 58
      among African Americans, 62
  political agendas impair research to
    prevent, 34
  con, 57
  risk for acquiring, 10
  and other STDs, 45, 75–76
  transmission of
    and gay sexual behavior, 72–74,
      78–79
    and viral load, 74–75
  virus in pre-ejaculatory fluid, 24
  see also AIDS
*How To Talk With Your Teen About The
  Facts Of Life* (Planned Parenthood), 26
human papillomavirus (HPV), 23–24
  prevalence of, 47
  in women's secretions, 25

intercourse
  alternatives to, 17–18
intravenous drug users, 51, 81
  HIV testing of, should be anonymous,
    62
  link with gay community in HIV
    spread, 77, 78

Judson, Frank, 51

Kaiser Family Foundation, 8
Kitasei, Hilary Hinds, 44

Latinos, 10
  HIV testing among, 62
lesbians
  need for outreach to, 48
  teenage, sex education should be
    relevant to, 33
Los Angeles Times, 50

masturbation, 22
  as alternative to intercourse, 17–18
  definition of, 23
  mutual, 23
    leads to penetrative sex, 27
Medical Institute for Sexual Health, 22

needle exchange, 54
Newton, Esther, 76

nitrate inhalants, 76–77

Obstetrics and Gynecology, 27
outercourse, 17–18, 23
Over, Mead, 45

pelvic inflammatory disease, 10, 45
Perez, Jorge, 52, 53
Planned Parenthood Federation of
  America, 13
pregnancy
  among teens in U.S., 38
  can happen without vaginal sex, 25
  condoms do not prevent, 40

Reiss, Ira, 38
Rotello, Gabriel, 56, 70, 83

safer sex practices
  benefits of, 14
  can make sex more satisfying, 20
  definition of, 14–17
  have halted AIDS epidemic, 83–85
  may spread STDs, 22–28
Santine, Manuel, 53
sex clubs/bathhouses, 80, 81
sex education
  abstinence only, is not effective, 32–35
    con, 30–31
  on condom use is not effective, 41
  must be relevant to sexually active
    teens, 33
  sends wrong message to youth, 27, 31
    con, 34
sexual abuse, 38
Sexual Ecology (Rotello), 56, 83
Sexuality Information and Education
  Council of the U.S. (SIECUS), 25, 38
sexually transmitted diseases (STDs)
  abstinence education can prevent,
    30–31
  costs of, 10–11
  dangers from, 10, 13
  increase risk for HIV, 45
  means of transmission, 16
  prevalence of, 9
    medical knowledge does not decrease
      incidence, 27
  prevention efforts, 44–48
  recommendations for combating,
    11–12
  research/prevention funding
    cutbacks in, 48
    is misdirected, 46
  safer sex practices may spread, 22–28
  testing/treatment
    confidentiality concerns in, 11
    name reporting in HIV efforts
      fear of is rational, 63–65, 66–67

unique identifiers are better
  alternative, 65–66
  will discourage, 61–63
  in women, 25
  bias against impedes testing, 45
types of, 8–9
Shilts, Randy, 77
Snow, John, 50
Solving America's Sexual Crises (Reiss), 38
Sonnabend, Joseph, 78, 83
South African Medical Journal, 24
substance abuse
  among gay men, 76–77
  encourages risk taking, 20
Sullivan, Kathleen M., 30
syphilis, 8, 18
  disproportionate funding for, 46

teenagers, 10
Thompson, James, 79
Torres, Rigoberto, 52, 53

van den Brule, A.J.C., 24

Weeks, Jeffrey, 81
Welfare Reform Act of 1996, 30, 33
Wittman, Carl, 72
women
  adolescent, HIV among, 38
  African American, STD studies in, 47
  are disproportionately affected by
    STDs, 10, 45
  bias against, 44–48
  counseling on condom use is not
    effective, 41
  public health policies are biased
    against, 46–47
  susceptibility to STDs among, 10, 17

youth
  HIV infections among, 37–38
  risk for STDs among, 10
  sexuality education should be
    appropriate to age, 33